A True American Haunting

As far back as I can remember, I was fascinated with the house on Brownsville Road. There were many great houses on that road, but this one—number 3406—was special. It held a strange attraction for me, even as a young child.

I suppose something had to have been at work even back then; why else would I stare at the place for years and imagine that someday I'd have a future there? I certainly had no idea I'd end up having to fight for it, to battle something so evil that it was beyond my comprehension.

Even when I bought it, other factors were at work. Through a twist of fate, as we were preparing for the move to Brentwood, I learned the house was on the market before it went up for sale. My mother was a retired real estate broker who still had contacts in the business, and she'd heard the owners were extremely anxious to sell. We jumped at the chance and they accepted our first offer without question. It took years before we understood why they did—and why they were so anxious to get out.

But by then it was much too late.

THE
DEMON
OF
BROWNSVILLE
ROAD

**A Pittsburgh Family's Battle
with Evil in Their Home**

BOB CRANMER
AND ERICA MANFRED

BERKLEY BOOKS, NEW YORK

THE BERKLEY PUBLISHING GROUP
Published by the Penguin Group
Penguin Group (USA) LLC
375 Hudson Street, New York, New York 10014

USA • Canada • UK • Ireland • Australia • New Zealand • India • South Africa • China

penguin.com

A Penguin Random House Company

THE DEMON OF BROWNSVILLE ROAD

A Berkley Book / published by arrangement with the authors

For information, address: The Berkley Publishing Group,
a division of Penguin Group (USA) LLC,
375 Hudson Street, New York, New York 10014.

ISBN: 978-0-425-26855-1

PUBLISHING HISTORY
Berkley premium edition / August 2014

PRINTED IN THE UNITED STATES OF AMERICA

10   9   8   7   6   5   4   3   2   1

Cover art: *House* © by the author; *Background* © by tuja66/iStockphoto/Thinkstock.
Cover design by Judith Lagerman.

This work is a true and accurate report of the events described. For reasons
of privacy, however, the author has in some instances disguised
or altered the identities of certain individuals.

BOB CRANMER'S ACKNOWLEDGMENTS

I dedicate this book primarily to my wife and children who endured this Hell and stood with me through it all. The leadership of Cardinal Donald Wuerl and Father Ron Lengwin of the Catholic Diocese, combined with the determination of Father Michael Salvagna and Father Ed Moran of the Passionist Monastery in Pittsburgh. In addition I give great credit to the steady and determined prayers of the devoted nuns of the Passionist convent in Pittsburgh.

Also, Connie Valenti, without whose spirituality and insight our efforts would have been exceedingly more difficult. Kerry Fraas who provided continuous moral support, and lastly, Ryan Buell, Adam Blai, and the students from Penn State University who did their best to help us.

Erica Manfred, my coauthor; Joe Veltre, my literary agent; and Michelle Vega, the editor; all who helped bring this book to fruition.

But most important by far, I owe everything to the Lord Jesus Christ, who died for me on a Roman cross, shedding His blood for my transgressions. "He loves each of us as if there were only one of us."—St. Augustine

ERICA MANFRED'S ACKNOWLEDGMENTS

I'd like to thank J. G. Faherty of the Horror Writers Association who generously agreed to mentor me on the craft of creating suspense, and who did a first edit of the manuscript, which was extremely helpful. I would also like to thank publishing attorney Sallie Randolph who helped Bob and me sort out contractual issues and work together productively.

Published by Trib Total Media, Wednesday, March 6, 2013, 9:00 P.M.

Evidence gives support to tales of local history in South Hills area

by Stephanie Hacke

A wooden cross at the base of a more than 200-year-old oak tree in Bob Cranmer's front yard honors a woman and her three children likely killed by American Indians.

Their grave, probably from the late 1700s, is verified by tales from those knowledgeable about the area, letters between leaders of the Northwest Indian War and a radar scan of the tree's base, said Cranmer, 56, of Brentwood, a former Allegheny County commissioner whose 1909 house was featured in a television documentary chronicling an exorcism he requested there.

Cranmer believes the woman's husband planted the tree at the property's entrance along Brownsville Road as a memorial for his family.

"It's pretty compelling," he said of the history he unearthed in his yard.

The Cranmers moved into their home nearly 25 years ago. It often attracts questions.

"People were always saying, 'Oh you live in that home?'" said Cranmer, president of Cranmer Consultants. "If you're from the South Hills, you generally know something about this home."

He was always curious about the tree. The home's former resident, Walter Wagner Jr., told him about a town legend that George Washington camped there.

Wagner, 78, of Bristol, Ind., who grew up in the home, said he is uncertain where he heard the tale.

"It just seems to be something that somebody once told me," he said.

Then a woman told Cranmer about the possible murder of a woman and children on his lawn.

She heard that Indians "killed and scalped" family members living there during post-Revolutionary War years, before the current home was built. The father, who was away when they died, buried his family in the yard and transplanted the tree at their grave . . .

Cranmer said, "Well, that's a pretty interesting story."

To find out if it were true, he searched the Internet and the National Archives, reading war department documents. He came across a letter from Isaac Craig, the commander of Fort Pitt, to Secretary of War Henry Knox, dated March 31, 1792, during the Northwest Indian War. The letter referenced the wife of Deliverance Brown, killed with her three children.

"(The Indians) wanted to terrorize these people from trying to settle out here," said Cranmer, a history buff. "Come 1791–92, this was a very dangerous place to be. I'm told this story and then I read this. How unique that in the same time period I find a record of three children and their mother being killed by the Indians." Yet he wanted physical evidence.

While watching The History Channel's "Unearthing America," he learned about a technique: holding two copper rods steady while walking above a grave will cause the wires to cross, he said.

Cranmer tried it on the grave of Pete, the family's cocker spaniel.

"It responded," he said. "So with that, I took it out to the front yard and sure enough, when I got near the tree, these things just started going crazy. It's almost like it's mechanical."

He hired Ground Penetrating Radar Systems Inc., a company The History Channel used to find a graveyard, to examine his yard. The results showed a man-made, 11-by-6-foot, disturbance at the base of the tree. The company's report said the findings are consistent with "an excavated grave site, with what appears to be the remains of objects four to five feet down from the surface."

"The images that were depicted would have shown four people buried horizontally," Cranmer said.

Cranmer's son, Bob Jr., 27, said he was "taken back" as he watched the radar experts in his childhood yard.

"Although, I'm not too surprised," he said, because he, too, has heard stories about the property over the years. "Older people would be walking down the street and see us on the porch and would come up and share stories with us."

Cranmer said he has done what he can to determine the history of the tree and burial site. He doesn't want to disturb the grave.

Instead, this spring he plans to place a brass plaque there.

PART ONE

CHAPTER ONE

Nothing in my background prepared me for the supernatural battle I was to fight in the house on Brownsville Road. Before moving there I'd had no experience or interest in ghosts. I never saw a ghost when I was a kid and paid little attention to anyone who said they believed in them. The only spooky experience I had was one day, when I was about eleven, my friend dared me to try to go into a supposedly haunted house. It was also on Brownsville Road, down the street a block from the house I eventually bought. It had sat empty for over a decade because it had such a sinister reputation. The big wooden door was painted white, complete with a brass knocker. I went up and knocked on the door tentatively and tried the brass handle a few times, but it was securely locked. I kicked the door as hard as I could, but it was sturdy and my tennis shoes didn't move it an inch. In a last-ditch effort, I turned away and walked back a few feet so I could get a running start. I ran up to try and jump kick it open like they did in the movies. Before I could lift my foot the door swung open on its own, with a menacing creaky sound. I didn't go in to explore. I wasn't that courageous. We were both terrified, looked at each other, and took off as fast as we could run. I later found out that the same evil deeds connected both that house and my own and were, in fact, committed by the same person.

Had I any idea that my childhood ambition of owning the house at 3406 Brownsville Road would eventually devolve into a nightmare, would I have taken my family and left right on the spot? Today I'd say yes, but back then I was so full of bravado that I would have bought the house nonetheless.

Ten years after I had packed up my car and headed off alone for the 101st Airborne Division at Ft. Campbell, Kentucky, I was coming home with a wife, four children ages four and under, and a large moving van filled with furniture. I had left the life of a career Army officer to move back to my hometown of Brentwood, a suburb of Pittsburgh. I loved working in Army intelligence and was disappointed to turn my back on a promising career and an assignment to Berlin, but my wife, Lesa, and I had decided it was more important that our kids could ride their bikes to visit their grandparents whenever they liked, so instead I turned in my resignation letter and took a job with AT&T Business Communications in Pittsburgh.

I would begin my new life by moving into the house I always dreamed of owning.

As far back as I can remember, I was fascinated with the house on Brownsville Road. There were many great houses on that road, but this one—number 3406—was special. It held a strange attraction for me, even as a young child. When I was in third grade, some school friends lived on the blue-collar side of Brentwood, and I would pass number 3406 Brownsville Road on a regular basis, going to and from their homes. Every time I passed, I would always pause and stare across the large yard with fascination. What was it like inside? The leaded glass windows, the big white pillars, and the ornate woodwork made it look like a castle. I wanted desperately to go in, to know the rich people who lived there, to sit in the living room!

I would later be told that there were reasons why I was drawn to this house. I suppose something had to have been at work even back then; why else would I stare at the place for years and imagine that someday I'd have a future there? I certainly had no idea I'd end up having to fight for it, to battle something so evil that it was beyond my comprehension.

Even when I bought it, other factors were at work. Through a twist of fate, as we were preparing for the move to Brentwood I learned the house was on the market before it went up for sale. My mother was a retired real estate broker who still had contacts in the business, and she'd heard the owners were extremely anxious to sell. We jumped at the chance, and they accepted our first offer without question. It took years before we understood why they did—and why they were so anxious to get out.

But by then it was much too late.

The McHenrys, the couple who sold it to us, claimed they were selling because Mrs. McHenry worked for the Pittsburgh School District as a nurse and a new policy required that she live in the city, not the suburbs. It did seem strange that they were moving from a house they had put so much work into. I wondered why she just didn't get another job. To be honest, though, I didn't care too much about their reasons, as I was so excited to finally own the house I'd longed for most of my life.

Like the house itself, Brownsville Road had a story to tell. Originally an Indian trail and later a plank-road turnpike, it had a history stretching back to the days of Lewis and Clark as well as the famous Underground Railroad. The road ran south to the National Pike at Brownsville, Pennsylvania. The first telegraph lines to Pittsburgh were strung along Brownsville Road.

At the time it was built, a few years before World War I, the house was considered to be a "country house," located about seven miles out of the city. Originally built by people of means, it was situated well away from the smoke and soot that dominated the river valleys. By the time we moved in, Brownsville Road was no longer an enclave of wealthy business owners. It had seen its share of both prosperity and hard times and weathered the decades in proud fashion, tarnished and faded in places but still fighting to maintain its dignity.

In a way, I identified with it. I'm a fighter, too. Growing up in Brentwood, you had to be. Sometimes you took your lumps, but you were proud to be from the neighborhood. You never ran away from a fight or a challenge.

The stately appearance of the house rivals any New England shore home or grand Southern plantation. The design was so unique it was designated as a Historic Landmark in 1994 and a front-page article about it appeared in the local section of the *Pittsburgh Post-Gazette*. Not as large in size as some of the other Pittsburgh turn-of-the-century homes—only fourteen rooms on three floors—it has an enormous front porch with large majestic white barrel pillars. It has a foyer the size of the average living room and an impressive two-tier oaken staircase that leads up to an open wraparound second-floor balcony. There are three ornate working fireplaces on the second floor and three on the first floor.

The house was originally built on four lots, but the current owners had sold off a horizontal lot in the back where the carriage house had once stood. A small ranch-style house had been squeezed in, and it looked completely out of place. Alongside the back were the neighbor's encroaching flowers, but closer to the side street and all along the side, the house was surrounded by tall weeds and vines and resembled an urban jungle. It was as if the place were trying to hide.

When Lesa and I first saw it, its sheer size intimidated us. The wraparound balcony on the second floor looking down into the foyer was something that we had never experienced before. The front porch with the massive pillars was also very overpowering. There was a somewhat seductive, stately feel that drew us in. The house exuded a feeling of history, wealth, and success. It was nothing like the small two-story home I'd grown up in, which was comfortable but solidly middle class. This house was a mini-mansion, and it fit my aspirations like a glove. I'd always pictured myself living somewhere really grand that matched my personality and ambitions. An amateur historian and budding politician, I always viewed myself as a general or a respected statesman. I imagined the conversations that must have taken place in its spacious rooms: the sinking of the *Titanic*, the start of the First World War, and the fall of the stock market. Windup record players had played music during the 1920s, and servants had once prepared and served dinner in an elegant, aristocratic setting. There was still a servant's bell in the kitchen. Minus the servants, I planned to bring it all back.

To my wife and our four small children, this house with its built-in bookcases, music room, and nine-foot ceilings was truly a castle. We could not control our excitement about living in such a magnificent place.

My elation was dampened somewhat during the walkthrough with the owners. Their behavior was strange, as if they were hiding something. We were down in the basement and Mr. McHenry was explaining the old furnace when Lesa suddenly noticed little Bobby was not with us.

"Where's Bobby?" she asked, turning around. The basement was partitioned into a series of different rooms, making it difficult to know if the boy was upstairs or hiding just around the corner.

"Bobby?" she called, "are you down here? Jessica, did you see your brother come downstairs with us?"

Jessica shook her head quickly while hopping from one foot to the other. "I don't like it down here," she said. "I want to leave."

"Well, honey, this will be our home soon," I reassured Jessica and then turned to Lesa. "I'm sure he's fine, Lesa. He's in the house, probably just exploring." Lesa frowned and looked toward the open stairs that led up to the door and into the kitchen. The door was closed. I wondered how that had happened, since I'd been the last one down the stairs and I hadn't shut it.

"You want to go look for him?" I said. From the corner of my eye, I saw Mr. McHenry glance toward his wife. His face had taken on an expression of concern, and he seemed to be trying to signal Mrs. McHenry from across the room.

Mrs. McHenry started quickly up the stairs and pushed open the door at the top. Mr. McHenry dropped the worried expression and went back to smiling.

"Maybe we've seen enough down here," he said.

As the door to the kitchen swung open, I heard a long and frightened wail. Lesa pushed past me and pounded up the stairs, with me close behind. We followed Mrs. McHenry through the first floor toward the massive oak staircase. As we came around the corner, Bobby's keening cry grew louder. He was sobbing hard, sucking in gulps of air in between the plaintive howls. It was as if he were crying out for help but had no words to express why.

Mrs. McHenry got to him first. He was standing in the center of the first landing of the staircase where the stairs made a sharp S turn, his mouth wide open in a wail, his eyes squeezed shut. Mrs. McHenry wrapped her arms around him in a tight embrace, hugging him close and looking around the room frantically, as if she expected to see something.

"Are you alright?" Mrs. McHenry asked Bobby. "Did something scare you? Did you go upstairs?"

Bobby was shaking, his usual carefree attitude totally vanished. He opened his eyes and his cries petered out, although he looked as though they could start up again at any minute. "You were gone," he said, looking up at his mother over Mrs. McHenry's shoulder.

"You got lost?" asked Lesa, relief evident in her voice. "It's a big house, isn't it? It's okay, we'll learn it together," she said, as Mrs. McHenry straightened up.

Lesa held out her hand to Bobby, who slowly moved toward her side. Mrs. McHenry took one last look around and said, "You really need to keep track of your children."

Lesa was not happy with her comment, but she took a deep breath and let it pass. She always tried to be non-confrontational and was better than I at not showing her anger. "You have several grown sons, don't you? Didn't they run through the house?"

"Not as much as you might expect," said Mrs. McHenry, as she turned and headed back down the stairs. As she neared the bottom she mumbled, "We weren't exactly told the whole story when we bought the house."

She was gone around the corner before Lesa or I could ask her what she meant. Her demeanor was so forbidding that we didn't want to bring it up later.

The McHenrys took us for a walk around the grounds. Mr. McHenry carefully pointed out where the property lines were, while Mrs. McHenry made short, angry remarks about the neighbor's carefully planted flower beds that crossed over into their—now our—yard.

Lesa pulled me aside and told me that Bobby still seemed frightened. He had refused to be out of her sight since she found him.

"Mrs. McHenry asked him if he'd seen anything," said Lesa. "What did she mean by that? She seemed really upset."

"It's nothing. She's unhappy we're here. That's pretty obvious." I was doing my best to calm her down, but I couldn't shake the feeling that something was wrong with the house. I finally attributed it to its simply being a big old house with cavernous rooms, but there wasn't the warm and fuzzy feeling that I had fantasized about. My hope was that once we'd moved in and added our own personal touches, the strange apprehension I was struggling with would go away. However, my unease was so heavy I sought out John McHenry and asked him to follow me back into the kitchen where we could talk privately.

"I want to buy this house," I told him. "I'm kind of a history buff, and I keep imagining all of the discussions that must have gone on in this house, the important events its inhabitants were witness to." I hesitated for a moment, trying to ease into my questions. "But you and your wife seem to have very mixed feelings about moving out of here. Tell me, is there anything wrong with the house?"

Mr. McHenry answered quickly, "No, no, the house is great. We're just sorry to have to go. But, the wife's job, you know." It was all he would say about why they needed to move so quickly and why they were willing to take the first offer that had come their way.

"We even celebrated Mass in the house," he continued. "Our boys had their first communion right in the living room."

"What? You had Mass in your home?"

"Yes, a few times." His eyes shifted away from me.

"The priests brought the Eucharist here?" I was confused, to say the least.

The Catholic Mass of Communion is rarely done outside of a church and only under special circumstances. The rite is considered to be one of the most powerful ways to purify and protect the soul through the transformation of the wafer and wine into the actual body and blood of Jesus Christ.

"That's right," said Mr. McHenry, again nervously unable to make eye contact with me.

His answer seemed very strange to me. Despite being raised Catholic and having been an altar boy, I had never heard of such a thing. But I figured they were devout Irish Catholics and it must be some type of Irish tradition. Years later I would understand all too well the meaning of his answer when we, too, as a family would attend Mass in that very same living room, and, for months after that, throughout the rest of the house on all four floors, including the basement.

"Can we get on with the agreement?" Mrs. McHenry's brusque question interrupted my thoughts.

The details of the sale took almost no time to complete, but we still would need a radon inspection done, the bank to send an appraiser, and to jump through all the other hoops that are part of buying a house. We filled time waiting for the closing by shopping for more furniture to fill the oversized rooms, and we were excited about a grandfather clock we bought for the foyer. We occasionally stopped by to take some measurements, but the McHenrys made a point to have as little contact with us as possible. We commented to each other on their standoffish behavior, but Mrs. McHenry had never seemed all that happy anyway, and we simply chalked it up to her odd personality.

Despite the way we laughed off the McHenrys' secretive ways, a continued sense of unease, of foreboding, still managed to creep into our thoughts. While I kept my feelings to myself, Lesa, a practical woman by nature, commented more than once about it.

"It's like the house is laughing at us," she'd say. "I feel like we're being taken in by it. We're not buying it, it's letting us in." One interesting "coincidence" made it seem that Lesa might be onto something with these assertions. When then owners prior to the McHenrys sold the house in 1979 they had a "house sale." I was in the Army by then, and my sister-in-law Donna went to the sale. I can remember feeling jealous when my mother told me Donna had actually gone into "my house." Anyway, she ended up buying an old crib that was in the nursery, and had subsequently given the crib to us when my son Charlie was born. The crib, which had been in the house for who knows how many years, was now headed back to the exact room she had taken it from. That seemed a little strange to me, more than just a coincidence. Later it would become a small piece of a much larger puzzle.

From the first, Lesa and I always had the feeling that we were not alone in that house, that we were being watched by someone, or something. I can remember the sensation so clearly. We felt surrounded by the past, as if we were almost living in it, that we were only temporary "visitors," tolerated for the time being—who would eventually be expelled.

Why did we continue with the sales process in spite of these feelings? I was driven by an assurance of personal destiny and the power of my faith. I had been drawn to this house all of my life, and just as I was moving back home to a great job, with a wonderful family, it went up for sale. We could easily pay what they were asking. I felt that it was meant to be, this house was waiting for us, and I was convinced that we were meant to live in it.

Besides, there is a big difference between feeling that the ghosts of history inhabit a house and an actual haunting by a malevolent spirit that wants to destroy you.

Moving day finally arrived, and we packed up all of our belongings. We had even bought a new car, a Chevrolet Caprice station wagon—the same kind of car my parents always owned.

"New house, new job, new car," I said to myself. Everything seemed blessed to me on that day.

We shook off the dark feelings that had been bothering us, and on December 12, 1988, we moved into the house on Brownsville Road, celebrating with the purchase of the grandfather clock that had a brass plaque mounted on the front with the month and year to commemorate our new adventure. I took a photo of our new home, standing back on the edge of the sidewalk where I had often gazed at the house as a child. Captured in the picture is my son Bobby standing on the porch, framed by the massive house. He looks like he's about to be swallowed whole.

Bobby had regained his playful personality after the incident on the stairs, but he was reluctant to investigate the house that first day, unlike David and Jessica, who roamed all over, exploring each room. When Lesa and I went to check on Bobby later that night, we found him curled up inside his closet sound asleep, instead of on his new bed.

I understood why the kids felt uncomfortable being alone at night in their giant rooms, and hardly a night passed when at least one of them wouldn't end up in our bed before morning. I, too, felt uneasy at night but decided that my faith would overcome any negative energy in the house eventually.

For the first month or so, walking into the house made me feel like I was walking into the inner bowels of a large oceangoing ship; completely engulfed by it. I would later come to think of it more like a Venus flytrap swallowing its prey.

One of our rituals became singing with the kids at night before bedtime from an old Baptist hymnal. One particular song that we always sang loudly and clearly was "There Is Power in the Blood." The kids loved it because I would stomp my foot on the floor to keep the rhythm. Even then, in the recesses of my mind, I think I knew I was preparing for something. What we were singing about so loudly and joyfully would one day become central to our lives. The sacrificial death of Jesus and the power of his blood would become our weapon against the evil that infested our house. It was a shield that would also become a sword.

Not long after we moved in, I was talking to a colleague at work who told me that his father had grown up in Brentwood during the 1930s and lived a few blocks from my house.

"So you bought the haunted house, did you?" were his first words when I told him which house I'd bought. I was a little alarmed by this statement, because by then I knew that there were issues with the house, but I didn't let on.

"No, I didn't buy the haunted house. That house is a block away and across the street." In fact there was a house on Brownsville Road that was known to be haunted, and it had sat empty since the 1950s. It was the same house that I'd been dared to enter as a child.

"My father always believed that the house you now live in is haunted as well," he said, going on to tell me that the house was empty during the late thirties and that his father and a friend had gone into it and were scared to death, and chased out of it "by something."

This colleague was a no-nonsense kind of guy, so I took him at his word and filed it away with the other things I'd been finding out. Little did I know at the time that I would later learn that there was a strange relationship between my house and the "haunted" one down the street.

Soon after we moved in, my mother suggested that I ask a priest at her church to come to the house and bless it. We were not Catholic at the time, but I'd been raised Catholic, and out of respect for her, I agreed to have her set it up. Her favorite priest at the parish was Indian born and his name was Fr. Victor. He was about as nice a man as could be, and he was genuinely happy to spend the time necessary to bless all of the rooms of our large house. He gave me a special bookmarker that he made himself with a quote from St. Augustine written in calligraphy which stated: "God loves each of us as if there were only one of us." I still keep it in my Bible.

He moved along throughout the house, stopping to bless each room without anything unusual happening until we came to Bobby's bedroom. Bobby was three years old at the time, and in a very determined, bold manner he stood at the door and refused to let Fr. Victor enter the room.

"Bobby, come on, he isn't going to hurt anything," I said, upset by his refusal.

"No, he can't come in. I won't let him." Bobby stamped his foot furiously and scowled.

"Oh, that's alright," Fr. Victor said, not wanting to make a scene, and passed the room. We paid no attention to the incident. Bobby was still in the "terrible twos" stage, and we assumed it was just a toddler's tantrum.

For about a year Bobby refused to sleep in his bed at night. He would go into his walk-in closet, turn on the light, and sleep on the floor. Eventually we just put a crib mattress in the closet, and that's where he slept every night, with the light on. From the first month we moved into the house and Bobby refused to let the priest into his bedroom, I had suspected that there was something strange about the room. I didn't understand why he refused to sleep in his bed and chose the floor of his closet.

The large room with plaid blue wallpaper, blue rug, and a beautiful fireplace would seem to be any boy's dream. But Bobby said that the room scared him at night and he felt safer in the closet with the light on. We offered to move him to another room, but he refused, insisting he wanted to stay where he was and just sleep in the closet. I knew many children his age felt there were monsters in their rooms, so I figured that he would grow out of it, and after about a year he did eventually begin to sleep in his bed. But as time passed I started to notice a change in Bobby's demeanor. Our bright, chipper little boy began to develop an introverted personality. I didn't associate this personality change with the "blue room" until years later when I would discover that the family who owned the house before the McHenrys would not use the room as a bedroom.

During our first spring in the house, I was planting flowers in the front yard and made an extremely interesting discovery. While digging with a hand shovel near the front corner of the property, I came upon a small metal box buried about six inches down in the soil. I dug it up and brushed it off and noticed that it didn't look like it had been there for a very long time. When I opened it, to my dismay, I discovered that it held a set of rosary beads and some religious medals. I called the McHenrys to find out if they knew anything about the box and why it was there. They told me very forcefully to just put it back exactly where I found it, refusing to elaborate further on the matter.

Soon, strange things began to happen inside the house. The first incidents were more of an annoyance. Every morning I would go to the closet underneath the massive oak stairs in the foyer to retrieve my overcoat. To turn on the light I would have to reach for the long, thin pull chain that hung just inside the door.

Every night when I came home and went to put away my coat, the chain was either wrapped around the light or meticulously twisted around one of the small screws which held in the glass shade. At first, I thought Lesa or possibly one of the children was pulling the chain too hard and letting it fly. But the children were too small to reach the chain, and Lesa assured me it wasn't her, so I tried an experiment. I left the chain hanging straight down in the morning and made sure Lesa kept the door to the closet shut all day, and yet, every night when I came home, the chain was wrapped around the light.

We told each other we had a friendly ghost in our old house and laughed it off. In order to solve the problem, I tied a wire onto the chain and wrapped it around a coat hook. The prank stopped, and for a while we forgot about it and went back to fixing up our beautiful new home.

Soon, however, the pranks would stop being funny.

CHAPTER TWO

Maybe it's not quite true that nothing prepared me for the enemy I eventually faced in my house. As a military intelligence officer in the Army, I studied psychological warfare, which came in very handy with a supernatural enemy as well as a human one. The personality traits I inherited from my parents were invaluable as well. Both taught me character and integrity and to be implacable, to never back down when facing an adversary. They were both extremely determined, somewhat stubborn people, which is what attracted them to each other, but eventually those same traits became a problem in their marriage. They butted heads a lot. When challenged, where most people would back down, they both would respond, "I don't give a damn what you think."

Neither of my parents graduated from high school, but you'd never know it from talking to them. They were voracious learners. My dad always drove me crazy correcting my grammar when I was trying to tell a story at the dinner table.

My father is my all-time hero. In addition to spending over twenty-five years in the Army as a military policeman, he chased bootleggers during Prohibition, escorted FDR, and even participated in an ambush set up for Bonnie and Clyde. Tall, handsome, and imposing, he maintained his military bearing in civilian life. With his squared-off face, stocky build, and jutting jaw he looked every bit the part of a lawman. Nicknamed "Cap," he was a John Wayne type, whose attitude was "bring it on" when threatened— that's if someone was foolish enough to start up with him. He was fifty when I was born, and I remember one day when I was twelve, and he was in his sixties, a young guy who was in front of us in a traffic jam came up to our car and started yelling at him through the window over some road rage incident. He rolled up his window and locked his door, but when the guy shouted at him, "You old jag off," a term no self-respecting Pittsburgh male would tolerate, my dad took off his glasses, got out of the car, and decked him with one punch.

A policeman appeared and told the poor guy to get back to his car. He then said to my dad, "Are you OK, sir?"

"I'm fine, but I broke my new pair of glasses when I took them off," my dad responded, holding up *t*... frame.

Cap applied for a position with the P... force in the early fifties after leav... because he wasn't from the comm... local politicians, and was a rea'... be easy to manipulate, the jo...

bricklayer. He eventually started a kitchen remodeling business. From time to time, he joked about his rejection, but I knew that it was a source of disappointment for him. Maybe that was part of the reason I tried to clean up the Brentwood police department when I became a borough councilman. The Brentwood police and their cronies disliked me intensely for it.

In contrast, my mom was the George Bailey of Brentwood. She sold real estate, and her office was a hub of activity in the sixties with Pittsburgh's exploding economy and the abundance of VA loans. A five-feet-two bundle of energy who never left the house without makeup, she was quite a glamour girl in her youth and loved to ride horses but could also wrap men around her little finger if she cared to. She worked all day, had dinner on the table every night, and still had time to bake little gingerbread men for me. Like George Bailey in *It's a Wonderful Life*, she used her job as a personal mission to help others. I remember one family who couldn't qualify for a loan because their finances were too screwed up. She managed their finances and paid their bills for six months, got them on their feet, and then helped them get a mortgage.

While my dad was the disciplinarian, my mom believed in teaching us lessons rather than punishing us. One time when I was a kid, I accepted some baseball cards a friend [sto]le from a store and my mother heard me bragging [about] it to my brother. She handed me a dollar and told [me to go] back into that store and pay for them. I was [mortified whe]n I had to explain to the salesclerk what had [happened. I learne]d a valuable lesson that day. I wish I'd been able to handle it the same way when my son Bobby stole from a store for some older kids and got caught. I spanked him and grounded him for weeks in the summertime. I thought, at the time, I was doing the right thing, but when I remember my mom, I still feel ashamed of myself.

Both of my parents had hardscrabble childhoods during the Depression. Like many people who grew up during that era, they vowed to bring up their own children so we'd never know what poverty felt like. With only three children, my two older brothers, Gene and Wesley, and me, our family was the smallest in the neighborhood, and we were generally the envy of the street. Our house had a swimming pool, we always had two cars, and every year we would go on vacation to Canada for three weeks and take two or three of our friends with us. I wouldn't exactly call it a life of privilege, but we didn't want for much. I wouldn't trade my childhood for the world.

My mom was a Catholic and a regular churchgoer who tried to instill a love of God in me. My father, on the other hand, had no time for any church, especially the Catholic Church. He would go with us on Christmas and Easter but generally mocked the long robes, big hats, and little cans with smoke coming out of them. "Give me your money and I'll save your ass," he would say. We would laugh and my mother would tell him to be quiet.

In the 1970s, when I was a teenager, Brentwood became a very wild and unruly neighborhood. The town gained a reputation of being a tough community that outside teenagers didn't want to venture into. What was probably one of the first teen drive-by shootings in Pittsburgh occurred on Brownsville Road when a sixteen-year-old was shot down in cold blood by other kids in a passing car with a shotgun. The boy that was killed hadn't even been their target.

Despite how well I was raised and how much I enjoyed my childhood, I became almost as wild as the community's reputation. I stole, got into fights, and went on drunken binges in high school, not caring much about anything. Formerly a good student at the Catholic school that I attended through eighth grade, I felt totally alienated at Brentwood High, a typical suburban assembly-line school, in my opinion an impersonal place that turned out "student widgets." During my four years there I can recall only one teacher, Mr. Paparella, who recognized me as an individual and tried to nurture my intelligence. Like many kids who are intelligent but don't fit the mold, I wasn't good at taking standardized tests. I gave up on applying myself when I figured out I was bright enough to do nothing and still pass with a "C." Good enough, I thought. I got in with a tough group of kids from the rough side of town and was transformed into a rebellious "what the fuck are you looking at" type of hoodlum. We drank regularly, shaved our heads (at a time when boys wore long hair), and dressed like bums.

On the first day of school in eleventh grade we actually went to the Goodwill store to buy old ill-fitting clothes, started drinking at 6:30 A.M., and went to school drunk. I quickly became a really out-of-control kid, and my parents didn't know what to do with me. Soon the local police officers knew me by name. As far as religion went, it certainly wasn't anything I thought about anymore, and I quit going to weekly Mass. My attitude was, science had it all figured out, God is a superstition, and if that's the case, who's to say what's right and what's wrong? I began to steal things like metal and auto parts for resale because it made me feel like a grown-up.

I was headed for disaster until a fateful day in 1973. My oldest brother, Gene, had come home to live with us after his marriage had fallen apart. He was really going through a rough time until one day he announced that he "knew Jesus." He had been "saved"! Unlike my brother Wes, who was five years older than me and always liked to torture me, Gene, six years older than me, was the eldest and had been a model big brother. He taught me to catch, helped me with my paper route, and encouraged me to work hard. In contrast to my wavy hair, when I wasn't shaving it off, and fair-skinned good looks (or so I was told when I briefly modeled clothes for kids' ads), Gene was skinny, with tightly matted black hair. In the early seventies, well before the evangelical movement exploded out of the South, and in a thoroughly Catholic community, Gene's "born again" pronouncement seemed to make him a candidate for the nuthouse. But he made it his mission to save me from the grips of the Devil and the everlasting flames of Hell.

"Bob, you have to be saved," he'd say on a daily basis.

"From what, you goofy idiot?"

"Go ahead and laugh. You're going to Hell."

"Listen you asshole, stay away from me. You're all fucked up in the head because your wife left you. Keep it to yourself and leave me the Hell alone!"

He talked about Jesus like he really knew the guy. I really didn't get it and certainly couldn't see that it had anything at all to do with me.

I avoided my crazy brother for a few months, constantly telling him to "get the Hell away from me." But he persisted. So finally, one night, as I was getting ready for bed, he came into my room with his Bible in hand and asked yet again if he could show me something. That was another thing: He read the Bible all the time. I didn't think ordinary people read the Bible; it was for the priests. But then I'd never looked at one voluntarily in my life.

"You have fifteen minutes to give me your pitch, but only if you'll agree to leave me alone after this," I said, totally fed up.

"That's all I'm asking for. Just listen to these passages."

So he opened his Bible and began to read to me from the scriptures, telling me who Jesus was and what he was all about. I was amazed. It was all there in black and white, not written in some code, easy to comprehend, and best of all it made perfect sense to me. I had read the Bible in Catholic school as a kid, but it was just words back then. Even when my mom told me that God loved me, it didn't really mean anything to me. Reading the Bible with Gene brought it to life. So after about two hours I could see that my brother wasn't really crazy after all. Goofy, yes, but still sane.

"Bob, Jesus loves you and wants to be part of your

life," he said urgently, as if convincing me was a matter of life and death. "He died for you and paid the price. All you have to do is ask Him. Go ahead, ask Him and see what happens."

So I thought, why not? It will be interesting to see if anything really happens. That night I asked Jesus to come into my life—into me, really. It's hard to explain, but where there was nothing, all of a sudden there was something. He came into me just as Gene had said that He would.

I had left the Catholic Church behind because I felt that it had kept the truth from me. I didn't realize at the time it had built in me a foundation of faith that I didn't even know was there. Growing up Catholic, religion had seemed like work. To be a good Catholic you had to go to Mass and pray, pretend to listen to boring sermons, be well behaved, kneel up straight, and follow the rules. What grabbed me about Gene's message was that the true meaning of the gospel was "You don't have to do anything. Jesus will come into you if you ask, and He already did all the work." Since then I've come to understand that it's not about churches, it's about Jesus. To me, He's as real as your next-door neighbor, and you don't have to go to a church to find Him. He came and found me one night in my bedroom. I can remember saying over and over, "What a deal! How could anyone pass this up?"

Now did I all of a sudden begin "praising Jesus" and stop drinking and cursing several times in every sentence? No, but a seed of faith had been planted that kept growing. In initially accepting the "deal" with Jesus that night, I had no real idea what I was agreeing to, or getting involved with, but I eventually began to read the Bible, too, and Gene and I found a Baptist church about a half hour drive from our home where people actually brought Bibles to church with them. Slowly and steadily my life began to change—not willingly or by design; I just became uncomfortable with certain aspects of it. But I still couldn't or wouldn't give up my wild ways. When I would try to stay at home instead of going out to party and getting into trouble, my friends would call me a "Jesus freak," which I didn't like. A lot of the time I wanted to be cool much more than I wanted to be saved.

I wrestled with this dilemma for over two years until one night in May 1975. My buddies and I decided to drive down to Pittsburgh where Brentwood's senior prom was taking place on a party liner boat cruising the rivers. After drinking beer all night, we drove to a bridge over the Monongahela River and proceeded to urinate on the open deck of the prom-goers' boat as it passed underneath.

"Get lost, losers," they yelled up at us.

"Fuck you, assholes," we yelled back, laughing hysterically.

Then, one of my friends smashed the large plate glass window of the furniture store we were parked in front of. It was about 2:00 A.M., the burglar alarm was ringing, and we had a flat tire. I didn't want to wait for my friend to change it because I knew the Pittsburgh police would get there first and they didn't play games. It was my belief they would crack your head open in an instant, unlike the police in Brentwood. I took off running and soon found myself walking alone, about six miles from home.

Even though it was a spring night, I felt cold with just my T-shirt, tattered bell-bottom jeans, and no jacket. I was in the mill district and had no money and little hope of getting a ride on those deserted streets. Despite feeling embarrassed about my predicament, I began to pray: "Dear Jesus, do you think that maybe you can help me out of this fix I'm in?" As I walked alone in the dark next to the towering J&L Steel Mill, suddenly a two-door Buick with two very large men in the front seat approached. I held out my thumb. I was nervous but relieved that someone had actually stopped to pick me up. I got in the backseat when the door opened.

"I'm going to Brentwood," I said, but neither man turned around to look at me. There was no conversation, no questions, and I began to feel uneasy as they quietly talked to each other at a level I couldn't hear. These two guys were so big that their shoulders touched in the front bucket seats. And what was even weirder was that they both had on the same loose-fitting Hawaiian-flower print shirt. As we drove, they continued to talk to each other as if I wasn't in the car. I became more and more frightened of these two giants in their strange shirts, my tough-guy façade completely gone. When they finally reached the border of Brentwood and the City, one of them simply said, "This is where you get out," and I did, quickly! The door closed and they made a left-hand turn off of Brownsville Road, which basically took them right back in the same direction we had just come, which seemed a little strange. Why did they go out of their way to take me home?

I was happy to be back in Brentwood, but I felt

terrible. The night's experiences were weighing heavy on me, and I remembered the night when my brother talked about how Jesus had died for my sins. Did He die for what I had just done? The answer seemed to be yes, and He still took the trouble to get me a ride home on top of it. I have often wondered if the two big guys were angels.

I stopped on the sidewalk silent and alone at three o'clock in the morning, and found myself in front of 3406 Brownsville Road, looking up at the house that fascinated me and would one day be mine. At that moment, I made a decision to change and start off on a new path of faith and learning, a path that would one day bring me back to this exact spot—this old, monstrous house.

CHAPTER THREE

From that point forward my life did change. I went to Duquesne University, made the dean's list, and did so well in ROTC that I was awarded a coveted "Regular Army" commission as a second lieutenant. I decided on the Army as my career. I quickly rose to the rank of captain and was stationed in Washington, D.C. Military Intelligence was my branch, and I excelled as an officer.

I met my wife, Lesa, on a blind date while home on Christmas leave in 1979. I had just come off a messy breakup with a girl I had dated in college. I was lonely and wanted to meet a nice girl, but that's easier said than done in and around a military post. So I did what I always did: I prayed. Lesa was only eighteen but quite the beauty, reminding me of Valerie Bertinelli. After our second date on Super Bowl weekend 1980 (Steelers 31, Rams 19), we went on to get engaged that April and married in September 1980. There was an element of providence in our marriage just as in the rest of my life. For some mysterious reason, from childhood, I'd always envisioned marrying a girl who lived around cornfields in the Midwest, and Lesa was from a little speck of a town called Upland in Indiana. She made my world come alive like nothing I had ever experienced or thought possible. We were perfect for each other. We shared the same values, the same desire for a family, and the same love of God. She also happened to be very pretty—petite and feminine. We also had the same desire to someday retire to a secluded home in the country with some land, horses, and a barn. For now, however, she was willing to put up with my ambitions and my long hours, take care of the children, and be endlessly support-ive, although sometimes it wasn't easy. My job in Washing-ton was demanding, and at the same time I was working on getting a master's degree in General Administration. I would leave the house at 6:15 A.M., go to classes after work, and then make it home around 10:30 at night. I was entirely focused on my career and school.

In 1984, we were living in northern Virginia when Lesa told me that I had to hear a visiting minister who was conducting a weeklong revival at the Baptist church we attended near our home. She had gone to hear him speak every night that week. It was Friday and I didn't have class, and it was the last night he would be there. I went to the service while she stayed home with our daughter in the playpen and our son in her womb. I'll never forget the tall, impressive young preacher with the deep Southern drawl who was from one of the Caroli-nas. His name was Steve Roberson, and his sermon was titled "Behold, the judge standeth before the door." It was all about living one's life in the fast lane of success, while ignoring what Jesus had done for us on the cross. His words that night cut into me like a knife, as if this man were directing his sermon toward me alone. I realized that the Army had become my god, and once again I was being called upon to make a change to my life.

I went to the pastor of my Baptist church in northern Virginia, the Reverend Harry Owens, and asked him what I could do in the church. Reverend Owens showed me an old school bus behind the church that brought children to Sunday school. "We try to get the kids to church even if their parents don't want to come, so we send the bus for them," he told me. "So far there are only ten kids on that big bus. Do you think you can fill it?"

"Sure," I said, and took it as a special mission to fill the forty-four seats on that bus. I set out into the community along the route, knocking on doors, asking if people had children who wanted to come to church. It amazed me that they would hand their children over to a complete stranger who came knocking at their door, but such is the Bible-based culture of the South. Soon the bus was full. I remember one day in particular when I had sixty-six kids on that bus!

In my wanderings I also knocked on the doors of plenty of black families and heard from white churchgoers more than one racial slur about "these coloreds" filling up the church. I asked the pastor if this was a problem for him, and he responded, "You bring anyone to this church house who wants to come." I certainly did. I taught

Sunday school, drove the bus, put on the children's Christmas play, and the Reverend eventually asked me to speak from the pulpit at the midweek prayer services.

The Reverend Harry Owens was a true nineteenth-century fire-and-brimstone preacher who inspired me with his fervor for the Lord. When he preached, he sounded like an Old Testament prophet. He had lost his right arm from the elbow down in an accident. He testified that he was a successful contractor but the Lord kept calling him to preach. After resisting the call repeatedly, one day he lost his hammering arm in an accident and finally took it as a sign that he better follow the call.

Captivated and motivated by Harry Owens, I felt that I was called to preach as well, so I started doing so once a week. Preaching in a Baptist church isn't easy, I soon learned. It's interactive and extemporaneous, and when you're not connecting to the crowd you know it. If they fall silent, your stomach sinks and you know you're in trouble. But when you hear a lot of people saying, "Preach it," "Tell it brother," and "Amen," you know you're on a roll. That's where I learned public speaking and how to read a crowd. I enjoyed myself tremendously during that time and felt that in addition to the Army, my second calling was to preach.

There's a saying in the Army that "if they wanted you to have a family they would issue you one." Lesa was pregnant again with our third child. One night we sat down at the kitchen table and made a list detailing all of the pros and cons of an Army life, and what we really wanted for our children. I fit into the military perfectly; in fact, many times I believed that I was "too Army" for the Army. But in addition to wanting to give our children the type of childhood I had experienced—with longtime best friends, vacations, grandparents, paper routes, and graduating with the same kids you were in kindergarten with—I was convinced that I had a calling to go back to the Pittsburgh area and have an impact for God.

It wasn't that easy. The Army refused to let me go. I got pulled back into service by my superiors, who showed up unannounced at my office to convince me that the Russians would win the Cold War if I left.

Then one morning I received a call that my brother Gene had been in a terrible car accident. I rushed to his bedside in Tennessee and sat there as he was dying and prayed to God to spare his life. I made a deal with the Lord that night.

"You spare his life, Lord, and I'll go home and preach," I told Him.

God didn't spare his life and I didn't become a preacher, but the Lord does work in mysterious ways, and I ended up going home anyway.

My parents were devastated when my brother passed. Gene had remarried, and his new wife and son moved back to Brentwood to be close to family. After the funeral I knew that I couldn't leave them. I made a special request for a hardship resignation that would release me from my assignment and I would say good-bye to the Army. The Soviets would have to be faced down without me.

I returned to Pittsburgh with the intention of becoming an ordained minister. I was already licensed to be a preacher. I went back to Library Baptist, the same church where Gene and I had gone, and to the pastor who had attempted to mentor me when I was wrestling with faith as a teenager. Pastor John Arnold initially encouraged me to look at becoming a minister and told me I could be ordained through his church. I started holding Bible study classes in my home, but support and encouragement from him seemed to wane as the weeks passed. Maybe he had the wisdom to realize I wasn't cut out for the job to begin with. Even though I was bitter and felt betrayed, eventually I came to the same conclusion—my mission would not be in the pulpit but in the public square.

After a few months, I realized that I had to move on with my life. I was on unemployment, we were living in a tiny apartment with three babies, I had no job, and no career. I knew in the back of my mind that I could always go back to the Army (officers were encouraged to reapply), but I was confused about this "calling" thing. So, in December 1986, only three months after I had left, I decided to go back to the Army. To my utter dismay I was told they were downsizing. Now I felt let down by my pastor, by the U.S. Army, and possibly by God as well. I had taken the leap of faith, and there seemed to be no water in the pool. I looked for work in Pittsburgh, but with the total collapse of the steel industry it was the last place on earth to find a new career. So I sent out résumés, and to my relief I received a call just two days later in early December from AT&T Bell Laboratories in Whippany, New Jersey.

Since AT&T was such a giant company, there was a possibility that someday we might be able to transfer back to Pittsburgh. To our delight, two years later, that possibility became a reality. With the profit we made selling our new house in New Jersey, we were able to buy the house on Brownsville Road for what seemed to be a steal.

I started thinking about preaching again. I wasn't ready to give up on it completely. I thought, "Maybe God was right after all, because here I am back in Pittsburgh. Maybe He just wanted me to pass through the Red Sea before reaching the Promised Land." So I became the young adults' minister at Library Baptist, at Pastor Arnold's suggestion. I did my best, tried to play the part of minister, but it just wasn't working.

One day when I was working in the yard a man named Jack Hartman stopped and introduced himself as chairman of the Brentwood Republican chairman. With that conversation I was eventually pulled into politics by the local Republican Committee. Eventually I made my first speech at a political rally and I was astounded. I brought down the house just speaking off the top of my head. My practice at extemporaneous preaching had paid off. "You write the sermon as you speak it," Harry Owens had taught me. It seems Harry Owens had not created a minister; he had created a politician.

Later that night I told Lesa, "I think I've found my calling. I can do this."

"I think you're right," she agreed.

Thus began my meteoric rise in politics. Within a few years I would be running a county with 1.3 million people—a good-sized congregation, I would say.

CHAPTER FOUR

I've never been afraid to go up against the powers that be, whether they're supernatural forces or local politicians and cops. But as a Republican in a town that had been controlled by Democrats for decades, and riddled with underworld corruption to boot, I had my work cut out for me.

On the surface, Brentwood was a great little community, with three grade schools (two public and one Catholic) and a junior-senior high school directly in the center. Everyone walked to school. There was a park with a large swimming pool, and the town puts on one of the biggest and best Fourth of July parades in Pennsylvania. But under the surface, and unknown to many, was a much more sinister side. Pittsburgh had always had a strong mob community, and its "bosses" were directly linked to those in New York City. A number of the operators of illegal gambling and the extensive numbers racket on the South Side of Pittsburgh lived a secluded, discreet life in Brentwood. Chester Stupak was the most notable. It was rumored that back in the 1940s he operated the longest running floating craps game in Pittsburgh even though he lived on Brownsville Road next to the Catholic church. Stupak also owned the notorious Lotus Club, a strip joint and gambling casino patronized by local politicians and other high rollers. I can remember one day walking home from school past his house and seeing a spotted leopard growling at me from behind the windows of a car parked in front of his home. What a mobster was doing with a leopard, I don't know, but I'm sure it embellished his already colorful reputation. His son would later become a famous Vegas casino owner, once coming close to being elected mayor of Las Vegas.

The good and bad money had followed Brownsville Road from the South Side of Pittsburgh to Brentwood as far back as the 1920s. There were two famous nightclubs that drew national acts such as the Lettermen and Buddy Rich. One of these clubs even had a large, well-staffed bordello conveniently located up a hillside right behind it. Another, the Fountain, was eventually torched mob-style and burned down to its foundation, killing the arsonist in the process. This was all common knowledge, and there is no question in my mind that the Brentwood police were persuaded to look the other way for decades. It was said that all five of the nightclubs in this relatively small town had connections to the Pittsburgh mob, and that didn't include the many taverns. No wonder they wanted no part of a professional lawman like my father on the police force.

I got into politics through a simple desire to improve the community I lived in. Brentwood's shopping center had once been a model for the nation. In the 1950s it was one of the first shopping malls in the country with a big downtown department store, Joseph Horne's, as the anchor. Not long after we moved back in the eighties, the center was deserted, a crumbling blight on the landscape. Horne's had closed, and as a result many of the other stores had been shuttered as well. The buildings hadn't been kept up and the center had gone bankrupt. Feeling that this was a terrible shame and that something should be done about it, I went to the Brentwood Town Council and to the mayor, whom I knew as well, to discuss the issue. He told me, "Become a Democrat, run for Council, and show us what to do to fix this." However, I wasn't switching parties, as I was a committed Ronald Reagan Republican. But I did take his advice to run—albeit as a Republican—and my political career was launched. It took a few years and election to another, higher office, but eventually I got a new shopping center built.

Although I didn't understand local politics, I quickly learned how things worked, and I put together a strong Republican committee and became chairman. We were facing one-party rule. I used my training in intelligence and psychological warfare to convince all the Democrats in Brentwood why it was necessary that they have a functioning two-party system. Eventually, I even had the Democrats sending us money. After I made my first serious speech and declared my candidacy for the Brentwood Council, people started coming up to me and saying, "What can I do? Let me work on your campaign. How can I help?" It was fantastic—quite an experience.

My campaign started with a bang, and not in a good way. In those days, the old party types would pay young guys to go out at night and drive around to take down all the opposition's campaign signs. I was out jogging one Friday night along Brownsville Road, and I saw three of them going from yard to yard tearing down our signs. I was in my midthirties at the time, and in good shape, so I went up and told them to stop. Before I knew it, I was fighting all three of them. I got beat up pretty badly and was hospitalized. I spent the next week there and required reconstructive face surgery. Of course, the Brentwood police never found out who did it.

The week prior to my hospitalization, the furnace boiler cracked, flooding the basement, the television blew, and my son Bobby's appendix burst. It was like an evil force was attacking us, and it probably was.

We had no idea how sick Bobby was, since he didn't complain of being in pain, which is very strange as appendicitis is acutely painful. Six years old at the time (1991), Bobby simply came down with a fever and began to throw up.

"I'm really worried about him," Lesa told me that night.

"I don't think there's any reason to worry," I tried to reassure her. "If he was in pain, he'd be complaining.

But just to be safe, why not call the pediatrician," I suggested, not suspecting anything serious was wrong.

She called and explained his symptoms, and the doctor's office phoned in a prescription, saying that if he didn't improve over the weekend to bring him in on Monday. The doctor said he probably had a virus and not to worry. But by Saturday afternoon he was worse and we found him out of bed and lying on the bathroom floor. He still didn't say that anything hurt, but I could tell from his color that he was very sick. We wrapped him up and rushed off to the Children's Hospital where he was immediately admitted. After a few minutes, the doctor came out and said that he was performing an emergency appendectomy because his appendix had already burst! We couldn't understand how he could have endured so much pain and yet said nothing. In retrospect I wonder if it had anything to do with the evil influence in his room that wanted to harm him. It was certainly in keeping with the personality change he had undergone since moving into that room.

After all this—especially my beating—Lesa pleaded with me to leave our strange house and this terrible community I had brought her to, but I was engaged in a political campaign and sincerely believed that I could have a positive impact. I had no idea yet how troubled Brentwood really was; that knowledge came after my election. I was seen as a "white knight" and was eager to play the part. Lesa couldn't understand this and obviously didn't share my emotional tie to the town. She was a scared country girl, and rightly so.

In the end I not only won but led the ticket, despite

being a Republican in a staunchly Democratic town. During my first few years in office everyone loved me. I put up signs telling dog owners to scoop their poop, I challenged media giant TCI cable to remove pornographic channels from the local cable station, and, with the help of Lesa, who later ran for the school board, we won a battle to stop the consolidation of all of the local schools. The honeymoon phase didn't last, however. I soon became a controversial figure when I discovered an illegal casino in the abandoned shopping center. It was like a speakeasy, with a peephole in the door. I was stunned when I just walked in and saw that the place was lined with illegal poker machines.

"What is this?" I asked the manager, genuinely shocked. "These machines don't look legal to me."

He looked at me like I must be kidding and didn't respond. When I left he waved and said, "Tell the mayor I said hello."

Naively, I told my story to the chief of police. "You gotta check this out," I insisted.

He became awkward and turned red in the face. "No, that's not my business. The county police deal with that."

Of course, I suspected they were possibly on the take.

So I called the Pennsylvania State Police who laughed and said, "Your chief obviously has a problem. It's his job to handle this, but we'll check it out."

They sent an undercover officer posing as a local, and the establishment paid him off when he won. The state cop said he'd never seen people so brazen. It had gone on for so long that the lawlessness was entrenched. I didn't know at the time that the criminal underworld was part of the culture and had been for decades. So the state police came back, raided the place, and cleaned it out.

After that happened, I sat down with the council and mayor and told them I was behind the raid, and that we had a problem with the chief of police. They told me to let it drop—to forget about it. So I went to the newspapers, told the story, and said that I was demanding an investigation.

Brentwood's Democratic mayor, James Joyce, wasn't pleased. He was quoted in the paper as calling me "very vocal, very abrasive" and claimed that I'd offended many of the police officers with my "calls for discipline."

Actually, discipline was the least of it. Eventually I found out that several members of our police force were drug addicts and alcoholics, and I went on a crusade against them all. In the *Pittsburgh Post-Gazette* I stated that "there was no discipline, no standards, no training, and worst of all no leadership."

While I was trying to do my best to get this rogue police department under control, the girlfriend of a police officer put his service revolver in her mouth one night and blew her own brains out. The police declined to investigate, and the autopsy report disappeared. After this I finally persuaded the rest of the council that the chief of police had to go.

A few months later my criticism of the police department was tragically verified once again with the death of Jonny Gammage, an unarmed black motorist who was killed during a routine traffic stop, gaining national attention. Gammage was driving his cousin's car, a cousin who happened to be a Pittsburgh Steeler. He was asphyxiated while being restrained by the officers on the scene.

In 1995, one of the officers was acquitted of involuntary manslaughter, and the trial of two others was ruled a mistrial, but the racially charged case—all the officers were white, as were the jurors—provoked widespread outrage and left deep wounds in Pittsburgh. The new chief refused to whitewash the Gammage incident, so the council eventually fired him.

We had a closed-door meeting after the incident, and all the solicitor discussed was our insurance liability. No one was concerned about the police involvement and what had occurred.

"I told you we needed to get this department under control, and now we have a dead body," I said indignantly.

"It was Gammage's fault. He shouldn't have resisted the police when they told him to get out of the car," said one council member.

"This was a human being, somebody's son, somebody's brother," I yelled. "And now he's dead and you talk about it like he's a dog hit by a car in the street. I'm not worried about insurance liability. I'm worried about these cops." I stormed out.

Pittsburgh exploded. Black churches demonstrated; Jesse Jackson came to town. Gammage's death and the lack of justice served on his behalf became a polarizing civil rights issue.

It was ten days from the election, and I was now running for Allegheny County commissioner. I was interviewed repeatedly and told the press that "I've been struggling with this police department for four years. I don't know what happened, but what I do know is that a young man is dead and should not be. He did nothing to warrant this."

A few days later, about two hundred people from Brentwood came to our house and rallied on Brownsville Road against me and my nonsupport of the Brentwood police. We had armed security in the house, and I slept with a shotgun under our bed. Our home was stoned and egged daily. I became a pariah in my own hometown of Brentwood.

One morning during the days that followed, I was feeling quite low, assuming that this huge controversy a week or so before the election would probably not help my chances. I took my Bible in hand, got on my knees, and asked for a message of wisdom. I opened the book to a random page and immediately saw a verse in the Book of Isaiah that gave me the strength I was looking for.

Later that evening my running mate and I were scheduled to greet a convention of ministers at a Pittsburgh Pentecostal church. The pastor, Joseph Garlington, was a remarkable preacher who was rapidly gaining fame as a founder of the Promise Keepers movement.

After my short greeting, the Reverend Garlington called me back to the altar and said to the congregation, "God has given me a message that this courageous young man needs our prayers to protect and encourage him against the forces of evil in our community." He called some ministers up and four of them formed a circle around me and laid their hands upon my head and shoulders. The Reverend Garlington began to pray that I needed protection and strength, and to my utter astonishment, he began to recite the very same verse from the Book of Isaiah that I had read that morning.

"So do not fear, for I am with you; do not be dismayed, for I am your God. I will strengthen you and help you; I will uphold you with my righteous right hand. All who rage against you will surely be ashamed and disgraced; those who oppose you will be as nothing and perish."

I was overwhelmed and began to shake as he spoke the words.

I tried to tell him that I had already been given those same words of encouragement, but by then the whole place was clapping and cheering. I hugged him, thanked him, and left, more determined than ever that I was walking a path that had been laid out for me by God Almighty.

The black vote turned the tide for me the following week, and I won the election. I was the first Republican in this heavily Democratic county to gain control of the county commission since 1932. To this day I'm a hero in the African American communities of Pittsburgh, and I attribute my historic win to them.

I didn't realize it at the time, but the evil in the house had begun to assert itself during my political career when I was rarely at home. In 1995, Lesa and I moved into Bobby's room, known as the "blue room," because I'd undertaken a major restoration of the master bedroom in my spare time, and Bobby moved into another room. Lesa had been a multitasker and a rock of stability from the beginning of our marriage. Despite having four small children to keep her busy, I could always depend on her to accomplish whatever I didn't have the time to do or simply couldn't do. She managed our budget, and when I entered local politics she was my right arm. When I became chairman of the local Republican Party committee, she became the treasurer. When I was elected to the borough council, she ran for the school board and eventually was elected president of the board. She managed door-to-door campaigns, political mailers, and fund-raisers like the annual pancake breakfast. She went to the state capitol to argue against the closing of our local elementary school with the Department of Education and later personally lobbied Governor Tom Ridge to reverse the policy, which he eventually did. Even though she hadn't graduated from college because I'd married her and whisked her off to the military when she was nineteen, she was a very bright, articulate, and beautiful young woman.

We'd always been very close and had a strong emotional and physical connection. We really enjoyed each other tremendously from the beginning of our relationship. Then all of a sudden she was frozen and cut herself off from me. It was weird, and the timing of these changes in our relationship corresponded directly with our moving into the blue room.

Lesa slowly stopped taking care of the house, and it soon became a mess. She got to the point where she couldn't remember to do the most menial of tasks. She had never had a hint of any psychological issues, and I simply thought that the pressures of the school board were wearing her down. At my prompting, she resigned, but things didn't improve. They only seemed to get worse. Finally, one day, out of complete frustration, I told her to take the kids and go to the lake cottage we owned about eighty miles north of Pittsburgh for some downtime. I would join her there in a few days. That night, as I lay in bed, I couldn't help but think that there was something terribly wrong with her. Looking for clues to her mental state, I got up and began to search the room. I didn't know what I was looking for, but after a few minutes I found a large box filled with envelopes hidden in the closet. I took it out and began to go through it. To my utter amazement, it was filled with six to eight months of unopened bills and letters. For a number of years we had worked on our finances together. I laid out a budget, and it was her job to write out the checks and pay the bills. It worked well, but since I had gone into politics more of the responsibilities had fallen to her. I couldn't believe what I found! Judgments against us from magistrates, collection letters, and worst of all, foreclosure proceedings were under way for our house! She'd managed to pay the gas, electric, and phone bills, so nothing got cut off, but everything else had been ignored. We were close to losing everything, and I can't help but think that it was by evil design to get us out of the house. The first owners had lost it via foreclosure, and we were about to as well.

Initially, I got very angry at Lesa, but then realized that this was not the woman I knew. The next morning I called her on the phone and asked her to come home from the lake. When she got home I showed her what I had found and gently asked her what was going on. She cried and told me how terrible she felt, how overwhelmed, that she just couldn't manage anything anymore and couldn't deal with the pressure.

"But why didn't you turn to me for help?" I asked.

"You were busy with the campaign, and you were working so hard, too. I just couldn't face bothering you."

"Then why not talk to Mum?" I said, referring to my mother, since Lesa and she were so close.

"She was helping you with the campaign," Lesa said despairingly. "I couldn't add to her responsibilities, either."

"Wasn't there anyone you could turn to?" I couldn't believe she'd been that isolated. She'd been on the school board; she knew local people.

"Bobby, you know I have no friends here," she said with a pained expression. "You don't know what it's like for us to live here now in Brentwood. You're always gone. I had no one to turn to, and I just couldn't manage it all by myself anymore."

At the time, we had no idea how much living in that house and sleeping in the blue room had contributed to her breakdown. She was under real pressure, but there was also the evil oppression of our own home. She eventually realized that now just being in the house made her feel paralyzed, unable to do anything. She'd forced herself to get up to do what she absolutely had to, to take care of the kids, but everything else—including the bills—went by the wayside. She didn't fully understand the role the house played in her breakdown until years later when the children were also affected psychologically. At the time she just took the blame on herself.

I called my mother, and for the next few days she and I

assessed the damage. My mother was a saint and helped me devise a plan to rescue the situation without bankruptcy. My family's financial stability was a major public relations concern. If the Pittsburgh media got wind of it, and I was astonished that they hadn't, the situation would have exploded into a huge scandal. But Lesa's state of mind was another issue. Through the help of a close trusted friend I took her to one of the leading psychiatrists in the city, and she spent the next two weeks in the hospital. Over the next year, she returned to normal, but her eventual recovery also happened to coincide with our moving back into the master bedroom and out of Bobby's bedroom. I had no idea at the time that there was any connection, but I would put the two events together later, as she slowly returned to her former self and once again became my trusted right arm.

My win for commissioner of Allegheny County had been nothing less than historic. There hadn't been a Republican board of commissioners in Allegheny County since Roosevelt won the presidency. I was the guy who as county Republican chairman had pulled the party together and did what supposedly couldn't be done.

I might have been a hero to some, but not to my kids. I heard a lot of complaints from them like "You go off and do all this important stuff and we have to live in Brentwood where everyone hates you. They hate us, too." We moved them to the local Catholic school, but even there they got bullied. Lesa invited Bobby's whole class to his eleventh birthday party, and only one kid showed up—his cousin Joseph.

There was an incident one evening after I'd been commissioner for two years, when Bobby was roughed up by some teenagers who stole a Boy Scout knife from him that he'd just bought and was showing his friends. One teenager just came up and asked to see the knife, thanked him, and said, "It's mine now," and walked away. Bobby came home crying, told me who took it, and I went to get it back.

"What happened here? Where's the kid who took my son's knife?" I confronted a tough-looking teenager in an alley behind the large apartment building where all of the kids used to congregate.

"Whaddya mean, man, I didn't take nothin'," he responded, sticking his face inches from mine.

"One of your friends took my son's knife. He's just a little kid. I want it back, and I mean now."

"What knife?" He tried to stare me down belligerently. "I didn't see no knife. Why don't you get lost?" He was obviously hoping that I would hit him.

I would have loved to knock this kid out, since I knew how Bobby was being harassed, but I could see the headlines, "Commissioner Cranmer Attacks Teenager," and restrained myself.

Lesa called the Brentwood police, and a new young officer came and took care of the situation—very professionally, I must say. I was glad I'd been instrumental in getting at least a few good men on the force. Unfortunately, I hadn't gotten rid of the one who disliked me the most.

Later that night, that particular cop, who was the sergeant on duty, wrote a false police report stating that I had gotten drunk and harassed the teenagers. Then he faxed it to the three local television stations. I was inundated with reporters and cameras the next day.

To even the score, Lesa and I did an interview in our front yard describing how the town had turned on us and how our life in Brentwood had become a nightmare for the kids. Now that the police had fabricated this latest event (I was also being sued in federal court by the same officer for defamation—a case that was later dismissed), we decided that we had to move. It was impossible, however, to sell the house in the middle of all of the bad publicity surrounding Brentwood, and we ended up staying. Ironically, the house being haunted had nothing to do with it failing to sell. Brentwood's reputation alone was enough.

By the late 1990s I'd gotten a lot done during my four years in office. In addition to changing the structure of county government to a system that functioned better, we cut taxes by 20 percent and built what's heralded as the best baseball park in the United States. We built the Steelers a new stadium and a beautiful world-class "green" convention center. Plan B, as it was dubbed, caused a tremendous amount of collateral development; it was a spark that caused a long-term ripple effect that's still transforming Pittsburgh. It's also the reason the G20 Summit was held in our new convention center in 2009.

The *Pittsburgh Post-Gazette* would later sum up my term in office in 1999 when I announced that I was leaving politics: "By thinning the field and working toward the day when Republicans have a single alternative to the policies of ill-conceived tax cuts, reactionary thinking and government-as-usual, Commissioner Cranmer has made the ultimate political sacrifice. If that is the mark of a citizen-lawmaker—to be honest, to spurn patronage, to reform the public sector and then get out—this commissioner has been one such leader. Allegheny County could use a few more Bob Cranmers."

Just when I was at the pinnacle of accomplishment, at the end of one particularly exhausting day I said to my good friend and colleague, attorney Kerry Fraas, "I think I'm done. I don't think I'm running again. I'm tired. I want to be with my family."

Since Kerry was the county solicitor, I was used to listening to his advice. We were both also men of faith, so on this occasion he told me, "Lay out the fleece." Like Gideon when he asked God for a sign to prove he should gather the Israelite troops to defeat the Midianite invaders, Kerry wanted me to be sure I was doing the right thing. Gideon put out a piece of wool overnight and asked God to make it wet while keeping the surrounding dirt dry. God graciously did as Gideon asked, and in the morning the fleece was wet enough to produce a bowl of water when it was wrung out. The next morning the fleece was dry and the ground was wet with dew. The fleece in my case was a political poll. To test the waters, I put on the best political commercial I'd ever seen. Then we did a poll and it came back that I was done. My popularity among Republicans had fallen because they claimed I'd cooperated with the Democrats and supported raising taxes to build the sports stadiums. (They were wrong about the tax hike, as we actually had the money, but I failed to convince them what we had done would transform the city.)

I'd taken a cut in pay from a middle management job at AT&T to become chairman of the county commissioners and manage seven thousand people and a three-quarter of a billion dollar budget. I did so much in such a short time, and all of a sudden I felt like I was being thrown out and abandoned by the people I'd worked so hard for. It was over, but now I know why. What would prove to be the fight of my life was waiting for me at home.

CHAPTER FIVE

Even with all of my ambitions and accomplishments, the most important thing to me was always my family. My four children would play an integral role in what we all faced within the house. We almost didn't have those kids. Lesa had some health issues that prevented her from becoming pregnant. After several surgeries the doctor told us that there was still only a fifty-fifty chance that she would conceive, and if she did, he recommended that we should have all of the children we wanted right in a row.

Six months later we were stationed in Arizona, and some friends who were going away for the weekend asked us if we would watch their three little children, ages six months to three years. We readily agreed and had the time of our lives with those kids over the next few days. When it was over we felt worse than ever; taking care of those kids just seemed so natural, and we ached for a child of our own. That week I prayed like I had never prayed before, especially for Lesa, since she had looked so content holding that little baby. Within a few weeks we were pregnant. In July 1983, right before my birthday, we went out to dinner to celebrate, and when we returned and pulled into the driveway I discovered a small miracle. Next to the carport there were some scraggly rosebushes that had produced a rose here and there throughout the spring but with the Arizona heat were now barren. To my amazement, as I opened the car door I saw one bush with one branch that fanned out into a perfect bouquet of thirty small roses. I pulled the branch off and presented it to Lesa, saying, "Here, this is from the Lord. He sends His congratulations!" That bush never produced more than a few individual roses again.

Jessica was our first child, and we naturally doted on her. She was an easy baby whom we could take anywhere. I often wondered what life would have been like if she had been our only child. Less exciting, maybe, but a lot calmer. As the others arrived, she was the caretaking child who became their "little mother." She was delightful and made friends easily as a little girl, but she was also sensitive and vulnerable and had to endure bullying as well. One time I confronted a group of five- to seven-year-old girls who were pushing her around and gave them a talking to that I'm sure they still remember. Growing up she continued to be our "low maintenance" child. I had big plans for her to become a trial lawyer, as she could always seem to best me in an argument with reasoned, sound, logical positions. After she started high school I enrolled her in an "Explorers" program with one of the large local law firms and got her a small position in a judge's office.

Bobby and I didn't get off to a good start, and, probably since we are so much alike, we've always butted heads a lot. He was what they called a "blue baby." They had to insert a tube into his lungs to extract birth fluid that he had swallowed during the quick delivery, and he was blue due to a lack of oxygen. They hooked him up to a heart monitor and said that he had to get as much oxygen as possible. I was so worried that I gently pinched his foot for a while, hoping to get him to breathe more deeply. So Bobby had a somewhat traumatic entry into this world thanks to me. Soon he was no longer blue but was red as a beet.

He gave Lesa a difficult time almost from the start. As an infant, Jessica would snuggle in with Lesa and nurse and was easy to get back to sleep. Bobby, on the other hand, was always a handful. She couldn't put him in bed with us but had to rock him in the rocking chair. Before he was six months old, he was regularly climbing out of his crib and lowering himself down to the floor. I would take a piece of terrycloth and actually tie a loose loop around his ankle at night, attaching it to a rail on his crib just to keep him from climbing out. Thus would begin the contest each night to see if he could manage to get the loop off over his little foot with the big toe of his free foot. On the few occasions when he was successful in accomplishing a breakout, I was forced to utilize two loops to effectively immobilize both of his feet, at which point he would rail at the unfairness of my move and eventually go to sleep. He had to have two bottles each night before he would even think about sleeping. We knew when he decided to go to sleep because he would throw his second bottle out of his crib and across the room. We'd hear it hit the wall, and so our nightly ritual before going to bed included the question "Did you untie Bobby and pick up his bottle?"

Unlike our gentle Jessica, Bobby took charge. We would see him in just a diaper and his cowboy boots out at the curb with boys eight and nine years old. They thought that he was cool, and as they would head off down the cul-de-sac on their bikes, he would steadily follow behind in his red fire engine, diaper, boots, and red plastic fireman's helmet.

When we moved to Pittsburgh he continued to be an older-than-his-age kid who rode his bike with reckless abandon, climbed trees, and constantly did flips and cartwheels to burn up his endless energy. An athlete in the making, he demonstrated why monkey bars have their name and had the scars to prove it. He always seemed to be the one in charge as the neighborhood kids congregated in our backyard. Prior to my entering politics, he had plenty of friends, but his best friend was his cousin Joseph, who was a year older than him.

He had his ups and downs in school but did average work overall. Even after he had to endure the harassment brought on by my publicity, he seemed determined to fit in. He joined the local pre–high school football team, but the coaches seemed to be biased against him because of their dislike for me. He refused to quit, however. I was proud of his determination and made it to as many games and practices as I could.

David has always been the most sensitive, vulnerable, and caring of our children. He struggled with a serious speech impediment, and we had a difficult time understanding him. Until he was about five years old, Lesa had him working with a speech therapist. From the time he was three, Jessica, for some reason, could understand him, so she would act as his interpreter. As the years went on, he sounded not unlike a deaf person when he spoke. This trait, along with his caring, emotional personality, led to taunts and ridicule from other children. As a little child, when he got upset he wouldn't initially cry, but would stand there for some time with his mouth open preparing to cry. We'd try to calm him down, but he'd still try so hard to cry that he'd turn red, then blue, and pass out before the sound was ever vocalized. We would always have time to catch him or tell Jessica to go grab him before he fell down. He did it so much that catching David became a regular thing until he was probably five years old.

Despite David's vocal disability, he progressed in school and was a good student. David's friends always seemed to be unpopular kids, often poor kids whom he would befriend. He led me to see the poverty that existed right under the surface in our own suburban community. That was David, caring for the unwashed and unwanted. When the kids would go away to church camp each year, David would volunteer to work in the dining hall and help set the tables. David could also never tell a lie, for his face always gave him away—it was as if he were physically incapable of it.

After David, Lesa decided that "three was enough" and scheduled me for a vasectomy. The day of the appointment she changed her mind and said that she wanted to have another baby.

Lesa knew that Charlie was her last baby, and they were very close. Charlie loved Batman and watched old original Batman videos from the 1940s when Batman drove in a black sedan rather than the Batmobile. He wore Batman costumes all the time and had Batman socks, Batman shoes, and a little Batman bike. One day a young couple came to the door and said: "Do you know that your little boy is up on your porch roof running back and forth with a cape on?" He had climbed out onto the semi-flat roof and was attempting to take off; luckily, he didn't!

One Sunday evening, as we were going to my parents' house for dinner, we had told the older three kids that they could ride their bikes and meet us there, but Charlie had to come with us in the car. He objected and cried, and we told him he would be older soon enough. They took off and we got ready to go. When we went to get into the car, Charlie was nowhere to be found, nor was his bike! We drove almost halfway there to find him pedaling along furiously on his little Batman bike (with cape) to catch up with his siblings who were now long gone.

David and Charlie were extremely close and did everything together. Neither one of them could get the upper hand on the other when they wrestled, and they would go on until I stopped them or they were both breathless. They slept together, ate together, took their baths together, and for years had the same friends. Charlie was a very handsome kid, as was David. They used to have me give them "bowl-cut" haircuts where the hair hung evenly around their heads with the sides underneath being shaved to the skin.

Charlie was also very close to my father, who was pretty much confined to the house by the early 1990s. Charlie would go to his room and talk to him and sit in his lap. When my father died in 1994, Charlie was six years old. He stood in the corner and cried, wailing, "Why does this have to happen to me?" When my mother died, he wrote the most beautiful poem about what she meant to him, which I read as part of her eulogy.

As a child, he was always coming up with sayings and words that he would take from movies and interject them into family conversations. Once I can recall him saying *au revoir* when he was three and putting us all in stitches. Another time when I had unexpectedly shaved off my mustache and beard he called it a "heinous act."

Charlie was the life of the party. He was very popular at school, as his witty personality was a hit even with his teachers. For his eleventh birthday we had a dance party in our living room with his entire class. He found a girlfriend at that party whom he kept into high school, but he had to constantly fend off the attentions of other girls.

He tried a number of sports—baseball, basketball, football—but didn't seem to have the interest or intensity required. Instead, when he was around twelve, he said that he wanted to take guitar lessons. We bought him a guitar, and he put together little bands until one day he became the lead singer doing professional shows at local teenage nightspots. Both Bobby and Charlie had musical talent and were in bands; however, Charlie also wrote and performed his own songs. One was a big hit on the Internet, and an agent once came from New York City to see his band perform live.

My kids have very different dispositions, and they were affected in very different ways by the evil presence in the house. Bobby and Charlie were affected the most, while Jessica and David still suffered but seemed to escape the worst of it, though they both had issues that may or may not have been related. Our children are so close together in age that they were very devoted to one another growing up, and this closeness helped them through our darkest days as a family.

I can't emphasize enough that my kids mean the world to me. What was to come was very hard on them and affected their personalities, and possibly their destinies, in ways that I can only guess at today. I've regretted many times putting them through the stress of my political career and the trauma of a house haunted by an evil entity. I often wonder if I did the right thing by them. I reassure myself that all in all, our kids wound up becoming normal, loving, and caring adults. Even though I was gone a lot during the 1990s, our bond had been well established, and we emerged from the next few years even stronger as a family.

CHAPTER SIX

For years we would experience things like all of the lights being turned on in the basement when we got up in the morning, and when we went downstairs to check the wood burner, occasionally the radio would be turned on and playing in my workshop area. The heating bills were so unbelievable I had installed a wood-burning hot water boiler to supplement the gas-fired boiler. On a regular basis throughout the winter when I would come down in the morning to check the fire, a chair that should have been at my workbench was sitting in the center of the room facing the wood burner.

Lesa and I would laugh it off and attribute it to our "Casper the Friendly Ghost." The children would tell us that they would hear walking and knocking outside of their bedroom doors in the hallway, and that it would wake them up in the middle of the night. We would dismiss this and tell them that they were dreaming, even though I knew that they were not making it up. I didn't know what else to say.

One night the kids had friends stay overnight and they still were watching television after Lesa and I had gone to bed. Across the dining room from the kids' TV room in the foyer is a five-foot "pocket door" that they had closed since we were upstairs sleeping. Bobby was coming out of the kitchen, which also leads into the dining room, when all of a sudden they heard pounding on the closed pocket door. He and one of his friends opened the door and walked into the foyer and said that it felt like they walked into a meat freezer. There is another door right there that opens to a set of "servant stairs" that lead to both floors above. It sounded as if someone were running down the stairs at them in the dark, so they ran back to the TV room and shut the door behind them. Needless to say, those friends never slept over again.

On another occasion one of the kids' friends said that he saw a misty black figure standing in the bathroom (through the doorway) as he was walking down the steps. He said that it looked like the "Grim Reaper."

Throughout the years these things would happen occasionally, and all I could do was to downplay them and tell the kids it was their imagination. I obviously knew different, but it wasn't like these were daily events, and again, it all seemed harmless at the time.

However, looking back on it all now, I can clearly see how the evil in the house was present, occasionally making itself known while surreptitiously working on us all mentally. As the kids grew older they would get into wild, almost uncontrollable fights that would rage throughout the house. I would lose my temper and fly off the handle over seemingly trivial incidents and would attribute it to the stress of all of my work-related responsibilities. But looking at it through the lens of time, not only did the evil in our house on Brownsville Road cause Lesa to have a nervous breakdown, it worked on all of my children as well, especially Bobby. We never suspected the depths of what was wrong with the house until we started seeing the evil manifest physically. During the mental attack that caused Lesa's breakdown, she never saw the presence that was draining her energy, but Bobby did, although we didn't find out about it until years later.

One night when Bobby was five or six he came into our room and said, "I'm scared. I hear a ghost moaning." I pulled him into bed with us, which became almost a nightly ritual with all of the kids. Lesa took a picture once in the morning that showed me and all three boys tangled up sleeping together, as they had all come in during the night one at a time.

Bobby stayed serious and withdrawn as he grew up in the house and slept in the blue room. It was his room for six years until Lesa and I took it over in 1994. As a little boy he would keep his emotions bottled up to the point that he rarely cried. He was almost like a little adult who would silently get angry and just look daggers at you. But unknown to us, he had had a terrible experience with the evil presence that he didn't reveal for years due to his secretiveness and because he felt that he wouldn't be believed anyway. That blue room was evil, and I now

know why the other families wouldn't use it as a bedroom. In Bobby's words:

*I was in fifth grade and I had stayed home from school
sick. My mom took all my siblings to school and then she
went to the pharmacy. I was in my room in bed looking
out the window. I heard a strange noise, something like
bagpipes playing. The noise got louder and louder and
then the door to my room opens and this thing comes
into my room. It was made out of what looked like
static, or lightning bolts, in the shape of a kid's body,
but with no face. It then seemed to hop or skip into my
room, stood at the foot of my bed, and then it went back
out the door. I stared at the door, and then this dark
figure, that I can only compare to the image of the
Grim Reaper, ran past the door. As I stared at the door
in shock, I saw a hand stick out with a black robe on its
arm. As I'm staring at the hand reaching into the
doorway I pulled my blankets over my head in terror.
Then the blankets were ripped out of my hands and flew
to my feet, folded perfectly. I looked up and there was
another figure floating above me. It was looking down
at me. If you took a human body and turned it into a
lightbulb that's what it looked like. There were no facial
features, just a lightbulb person. I closed my eyes and
screamed really loud and it all stopped. I lay in bed
until my mom got home but didn't say anything. I felt
total terror, like I was going to die.*

*When I later told the story to the priests they said the
small entity that came in first was a ghost or a spirit the
larger, evil entity in black had under its control and it*

was all designed to terrify me. However, the glowing
entity over my bed apparently was a guardian angel
that intervened to protect me and that ended it. The
whole experience was terrifying, and I didn't feel there
was an angelic being there at all. It was horrible.

Over the years, Bobby's account of his frightening
experience with the evil presence and his friends' sight-
ings would be corroborated. The shadowy figure dressed
in black would appear to every member of the family in
different rooms of the house. It was about five feet tall
and would appear as a "misty" black cloud or sometimes
a distinct figure. David described it most clearly as a figure with straight black shoulder-length hair, wearing
what appeared to be a black cloaklike dress that covered
its neck and arms down to the wrists.

Jessica, in later years, would wake up in the middle of
the night and be frozen in her bed, unable to move any
of her limbs. This started to occur when she was twelve
and we decided to move her bedroom up the servant
steps to the vacant third-floor separate living quarters
(we called it the apartment). She would eventually live
there with her son and husband. She later told us that
the paralysis at night would happen on a regular basis.

With this thing, there was never any pretense as to it
being some type of "lost soul" caught up in a tragedy
from long ago. This evil entity was obviously part of the
present and made its intentions clear that its sole purpose was to scare and terrify us, and it primarily liked to
focus upon the children.

The black figure also had another bizarre characteristic

that it eventually revealed to us. When it wanted to make itself known it would emit a stench very similar to that of burning rubber mixed with sulfur. This stench would move throughout the room or rooms that it was occupying. On other occasions it would use a strong smell similar to urine, or—as Lesa described it—the odor of amniotic fluid. Sometimes it would be a faint scent, and at other times it was so strong that it made us sick. It was always very localized, meaning that it was similar to a person with bad breath or body odor. You can smell it when next to the person, but move a few feet away and it's not detectable. When the haunting went into high gear in 2003, I would find the stench useful because I could use it to actually chase the spirit from room to room as it challenged me for dominance. For some reason this thing preferred to harass me with its horrific burning sulfuric smell rather than a visible presence.

From the late 1980s until the early 2000s, when I left political office, we knew the spirit was there but it flew under our radar, so to speak. For years I would be intrigued but not particularly threatened by its presence, and I certainly had no idea what it was doing to us mentally. Eventually it would become very up close and personal in its intention to either drive us out of the house or destroy us in the process. But during these earlier years it was impossible to see any method or strategy at work as it manipulated each of us separately and secretly. This was undoubtedly its plan, to attack each of us individually in subtle ways that we wouldn't recognize until it was too late—a plan that almost succeeded.

CHAPTER SEVEN

When I left political life in 2000, I went to work for a large architectural-engineering firm that did a lot of government work. It was a great job, but it was hard to accept, after all that I had gone through, that my political and spiritual journeys were now over. I had to come to grips with the fact that I would never move on to be governor, senator, or president—or become a minister. One day later that year when I was at work we had an older African American woman filling in as a temporary receptionist for a week. Other than saying hello I didn't interact with her much until one afternoon she asked if she could tell me something personal. I agreed, curious to hear what she might tell me. Sounding like a soothsayer as she spoke, she said, "I don't know you at all, and I don't know what this means, but I was given a word of wisdom for you last night. The Lord told me to tell you that you should just be patient. He's going to use you for something."

A day or so later she left and I never saw her again.

I needed something—some contact with what I had lost—but I wasn't sure how that would manifest itself in my life. As usual, providence led me to exactly the right place—a place that I had been visiting over the last few years that would not only feed my soul but would lead me to help when I desperately needed it.

A short distance away from my house is a somewhat mysterious convent that is home to a group of cloistered nuns of the Passionist order. I call it mysterious because as I was growing up we would look at the building guarded behind a wall and large black iron fence and wonder what was going on inside. You would never see anyone standing outside the convent, but I was told by my mother that it housed nuns who lived their entire lives there in complete seclusion.

The convent was built at the exact same time as our house during the years of 1909 and 1910, when the order moved to the United States from Italy. It is considered to be a very holy, almost mystical place where Mother Teresa of Calcutta had insisted on staying the two times she visited Pittsburgh.

During my term in office as county commissioner, I would regularly be given gifts of candy, fruit baskets, hams, and other assorted edibles during the holidays, usually enough to fill a small pickup truck. I asked a friend to whom I should donate the stuff, and he suggested the Passionist nuns because the convent was on my way home from the office.

I began to stop by the convent on a regular basis to drop off all of the food. It became somewhat of a joke with my staff as to what surprises the nuns would be getting that night! Once, when a particularly large basket arrived from the Pittsburgh Steelers with a six-pack of Iron City Beer in it, I removed the beer, but other than that everything always went to the nuns. I would enter a small entrance chamber, ring a bell, and a voice would emanate from behind a screen in a huge locked door. I would tell the voice that I had a gift, and a large circular metal shelf would turn open. I would place my gift in it and it would close. Sometimes this process would go on for a while, as I could only fit so much in the turnstile at one time. I would hear a "thank you" and that was it; I would leave. This went on for a number of months until one day to my surprise, Mother Maria, the mother superior in charge, actually opened the door to receive my gifts in person. We had a very pleasant talk, and she told me how the nuns were always so excited to receive my interesting, sometimes extravagant baskets of food and candy.

During Christmas week Lesa and I went out to the grocery store and bought everything needed for an entire dinner for the nuns. When we delivered it on Christmas Eve, we were invited into a small visiting area. Because it was Christmas week the sisters were permitted to come out and thank us for the food and all of the baskets they had received over the previous weeks. We began a tradition of attending midnight Mass at the chapel in the convent, and eventually we became good friends with Mother Maria and the other nun in charge. Even though we as a family attended a Baptist church, I also began to attend Mass each Saturday morning at the convent.

The chapel is separated into two sections, one for the nuns and one for the public, with the altar and a large open window serving as a divider. The spirit of God is unmistakable in the small chapel. I felt extremely close to God when I was there. I told Lesa that it was like a "spiritual bath" and I always felt energized and focused when I left. I would often stop by the chapel on my way home from work and kneel alone in solitude and listen as the nuns sang their evening prayers. As events in the house got stranger, as an evil force started undermining my family, my time in the convent chapel offered me solace.

Sometime during the year 2000, after I left political office, Mother Maria called and asked me if I would help clear their property inside the fence of overgrown brush and trees. I was excited and honored that she had thought me worthy to enter their world and took the job with a youthful enthusiasm! Whatever she wanted done, I was at their disposal. I was like a kid.

However, it turned out to be like the movie *Lilies of the Field* as she came up with task after task for me to accomplish.

Over the decades about five acres had grown up into a small jungle, and it turned out to be quite a job. I worked on their property for an entire summer during my free time, eventually clearing all of the overgrowth and cutting down trees. On a few occasions some of the younger nuns would come out into the hot sun and work with me in silence while I fed debris into a large wood chipper.

My next task was to build an outdoor prayer park with a path through the trees for the sisters, complete with the fourteen stations of the cross, all with six-foot wooden crosses that I built in my backyard. I also built a large arched brick grotto as part of the prayer park. My father taught me carpentry, and I soon found out that I was also a good bricklayer. It must have been the spirit guiding me, for when I placed the final bricks in the arched roof, it was perfect. And because I used "old bricks," it looked as old as the convent! It was placed just so that the nuns could look out of the convent and see it. They were so grateful and excited. When I finally placed the statue of Mary in the grotto it was a high point of my life. I still look at the grotto and prayer park with pride, and the work I did there continues to give me feelings of deep satisfaction to this day.

I enjoyed talking to Mother Maria about my family, my life, and spiritual things in general. I felt it an honor to have the opportunity to get to know someone who had dedicated herself entirely to a monastic life of contemplative prayer devoted to the passion, death, and resurrection of Jesus Christ.

Mother Maria seemed to be in her sixties and told me that she had previously been a member of a missionary order in Central America. She told me how she became familiar with the local customs of voodoo and black magic, and how the spirit world was an everyday part of cultural norms among the people there. Later, when directly confronted with evil in my own house, I thought of her immediately.

The Passionist order of Catholicism is extremely spiritual and focuses on giving oneself completely to God. Some Passionist priests also are involved in what they call "deliverance work," which involves using their spiritual authority to confront demonic influence, be it in a home or a person, and on rare occasions, actual demonic possession, which warrants a full exorcism. I truly believe the opportunity to know Mother Maria and to enter this closed mystical world of the convent was by design, or possibly divine providence.

Mother liked to talk about a wide variety of topics and related how, as a young nun, she had taught school in New York where a little boy named Mel Gibson had attended as a student before his family moved to Australia. She said that he was a handful but she thought the world of him. In 2004 his movie *The Passion of the Christ* would be released. I would later buy a copy of the video for the nuns, and that movie would play nonstop twenty-four hours a day for more than six months in our house. Mel's movie, or what it depicted, would play a key role when my battle with the evil presence was at its most intense.

CHAPTER EIGHT

It was a beautiful spring evening in April 2001, and life was good. Even though we had been dealing with some paranormal issues in our home for years, we were still a happy family. Somehow we'd managed to ignore the strange things that happened in the house even though they were always in the back of our minds. Little did I know that this was the calm before the super-storm. I had returned from an early evening event in a neighboring county and was looking forward to a relaxing weekend. I had left the stress of politics and government behind, and my life had a sense of peace and order again. All of our four children were doing reasonably well at the time, but my wife and I were particularly proud of Jessica, our sixteen-year-old daughter. Always mature for her age, Jessica was talking about becoming a trial lawyer and had been attending an Explorers program sponsored by a large law firm. Focused on her education, she'd only dated casually, but at the beginning of the year she had taken an evening job as a waitress and had met her first "real" boyfriend.

Lesa and I had several heart-to-heart discussions with her concerning becoming too serious too fast, and also addressed that three-letter word S-E-X. She assured us that she understood and guaranteed us that she knew better. We were quite confident that she did, and believed that we had nothing to worry about.

When I got home that evening I was feeling great and prepared to have a late dinner and then do some yard work. After a few minutes Lesa came into the kitchen and calmly announced, "Jessica has something to tell you."

"Fine, where is she?" I asked, and then got up to go to her in the TV room. Expecting a pleasant surprise, I walked into the room to see my daughter sitting on the couch with tears streaming down her cheeks.

Before she said a word to me, the first thought that entered my mind was "this isn't happening."

"I'm pregnant, Dad," she said. With those words I felt like I'd been hit by a sledgehammer.

Trying to keep my composure and still in disbelief, I said nothing and sat down. I wanted to yell at her, I wanted to ignore it, I wanted to blame her, but I attempted to discuss the situation as reasonably as I could even though I was numb. The deed was done and I had to accept it. My insulated little family had been violated. High school, college, the legal career we spoke of, everything now was in complete disarray. "What to do, what to do?" I asked myself. I generally could always come up with a course of action.

"We need to deal with this situation together, Jessica," I said, realizing that I didn't want her to have to deal with it alone. "We should look at adoption."

"I don't know, Dad. I don't know if I want to do that," she said, sounding agonized about it.

"There are an awful lot of couples desperate for a child who could give this baby a good home," I said. "We'll think about it and discuss our options later."

Jessica thought about it for a week, and then consulted my mother, who always seemed to give sound, down-to-earth advice.

"Adoption doesn't seem right for me," she told my mother. "I can't give away my baby."

"Sweetheart," my mother responded, "give it time and God will let you know what to do. Never do anything because you think it's going to make other people happy. If you have to give the baby to somebody you can just give it to me."

Jessica decided to keep the baby, and although I had a hard time accepting her pregnancy and hesitated even going to the hospital for the birth, I soon found myself falling in love with my first grandchild, Collin. He became like another son to me, and it was difficult to remember my initial anguish. As always with a new baby, he was the most beautiful little guy in the world. Light brown hair with big brown eyes and a funny little smile. What had been a mountainous issue for me soon became a spot on the floor. After Collin was born, Jessica started back to a regular school schedule, Lesa got a new job, and my mother watched him every day. She died unexpectedly a week or so before Jessica graduated from high school. I'm happy that she was able to spend so much time with her first great-grandchild. If it hadn't been for her down-to-earth wisdom, we probably wouldn't have him with us today.

Jessica was hoping to marry Collin's father, but he was just a high school junior who loved to have a good time, and had nowhere near the maturity Jessica needed. She eventually broke up with him, and she and Collin stayed with us. They set up house on the third floor with a nice, spacious nursery.

However, as Collin passed the eighteen-month mark and approached two, we realized that he wasn't developing at a normal pace. He could hardly walk and was making little attempt to talk. Jessica sought out a therapist to work with him, but we were concerned that he might have serious mental or emotional issues. In retrospect, I wonder if Collin's and David's speech problems were somehow caused by the same source, living in this evil house.

While Jessica was growing up fast as a single teen mom, Bobby was becoming more unruly and spiraling totally out of control. When he was about fifteen he began to change dramatically. Up to that point he had been the picture of the wholesome American youth: polite, with short hair, the handsome football player that everyone liked. Then overnight he quit playing football, dyed his hair a bright florescent red, and began to listen to extreme death-metal bands. Prior to his dramatic personality change he had moved back into the blue room, and soon the walls were covered from floor to ceiling with grotesque posters of various bands that looked to have been printed in Hell.

When Lesa's parents came to visit, they slept in his room over the weekend and were terrified by the experience. I told them that it was just a phase and that it would pass. I downplayed the changes in my son and attributed them to adolescent rebellion for quite a while. Bobby put together his own band with some friends, which apparently was quite good and actually played in some Pittsburgh youth clubs. But soon he looked like the pictures on his walls. Black clothes, black hair, black makeup, black fingernails, tattoos, chains, multiple piercings, bolts through his ears and lips—the kid looked like he came right from the lower regions. His whole personality changed in a way that went well beyond just being a rebellious teenager. One day when Lesa tried to get him out of bed to go to school he went after her physically. He'd punch the car and threaten to hurt people. He was once caught stealing a CD from a heavy metal record store.

David followed his brother but only in the way he looked. His hair was shaved on the sides and braided down the middle. But with him, the Goth thing was superficial and didn't last long. One night I said to him, "Will you please take all those goofy rubber bands off your wrists and start dressing normal again?" He took them off, stopped wearing all black clothes, and cut his hair. He went back to being David, but Bobby and Charlie got worse.

Charlie was sucked into the same heavy metal culture as

Bobby. He says he got into the counterculture because he claimed that kids hated him for his last name. I was bewildered by these changes in my kids, worried about them and at a loss as to how to deal with them. I was a take-charge guy, a strategy that worked at the office but not at home.

Soon it felt as though we were foreigners in our own home. By 2003, Bobby was completely out of control. He wouldn't come home for days at a time, and even though he didn't have a driver's license he would take the car at night when we were asleep.

Finally I said I was going to send him to a boarding school.

"Bobby, you can't keep this up forever," I told him one night in August. "You're going to wind up in the hospital, in jail, or worse. I'm sending you back to Kiski Prep when school starts."

I had sent him to Kiski Prep, north of Pittsburgh, over the summer, and it had seemed to do him a world of good.

"Fuck you," he yelled at me defiantly. "I'm not going back to that lame school. You can't send me anywhere. I'm outta here!"

We didn't see him for almost a week. I dropped that plan, and when school started he simply decided not to attend at all; in fact he wouldn't leave his bedroom. He covered all of the windows with blankets and would stay in bed in the blackened room or listen to his heavy metal music. When he came out he would leave the house and we had no idea what he was doing. It was at that point that I decided that this was more than a phase and that I had to gain control over him again. But it was too late.

One night he hurt himself so badly by cutting his wrist with a razor that we had to call an ambulance to take him to the hospital. We simply didn't know what to do.

While my relationship with Bobby had been seriously strained, we were still able to connect from time to time, and Sunday, September 14, 2003, was one of those days, which made the events of that night even more shocking. I had taken Bobby and Charlie to a Pirates baseball game that Friday, and earlier in the evening Bobby and I had taken a ride in a convertible sports car I had recently purchased. A few hours after we got home I went downstairs to confront Bobby over his leaving my bathroom in total disarray, with his clothes and wet towels strewn over the floor. He screamed, "Fuck you!" and in a wild rage began to attack me. By then he was no longer a child and in fact weighed about twenty pounds more than me due to antidepressants he was on. He knocked me down and began to pummel me and yelled that he was going to kill me. I noticed that he didn't sound like himself, his voice was very deep, and it was almost impossible to control his strength or the violence of his blows. We fought throughout the first floor of the house until I finally overpowered him on the kitchen floor.

At one point Charlie started hitting me as well, and then he jumped up and called 911, yelling that he was going to have me arrested. Even though Charlie was just fourteen at the time, calling 911 was something I've found hard to understand, since David was there trying to help me control Bobby.

When the Brentwood police arrived, it was a chaotic scene. Lesa was so upset that she didn't know what to do. I attempted to explain what had happened, but Bobby was lying semiconscious on the floor, and I was the one led out in handcuffs. I was taken to the county jail where the guards that had recently worked for me put me in a cell with two drug dealers. I spent the night, and in the morning I was marched out in handcuffs and leg irons and stood before the judge, who seemed to be more embarrassed than me, seeing the former chairman of the Board of County Commissioners standing before him in shackles. I was released without bail, and within a few hours the event hit the media. What had been building up for years had finally erupted, and I would soon be the one expelled from my own home.

The whole event seemed to explode out of nowhere. One minute I was getting ready for bed, and a half hour later I was in the back of a police cruiser. As for Bobby, he still can't make sense of what happened, either: "When me and my dad got into that fight it was the weirdest experience," he says today, "because the entire day was a father/son bonding day. We were having a great time and within an hour of being in the house we were ready to kill each other."

Just when things couldn't get any worse, they did. After I was released I went back to Brentwood by bus and had Lesa meet me with my car, a shirt, a suit, and a change of clothes. I had been ordered by the judge to stay out of the house, so I went to the downtown health club that

I belonged to, showered, got dressed, and went to my office across the street. When I got to my office, Lesa called me and gave me some more upsetting news. My eighty-eight-year-old aunt, who had moved in with us the previous year when my mother passed, was upstairs in her bedroom—dead! Her heart must have given out during the night after the excitement of the fight. I've often wondered if the evil thing that had launched this surprise turmoil hadn't played a part in the death of this frail, sweet old woman. The television cameras were outside the house filming as the ambulance took her body away, and a news helicopter was actually hovering overhead. I left work and went directly to the local funeral home to make the necessary arrangements. I was met there by a throng of television cameras and reporters wanting to cover the "big story." The event hit the Associated Press and even appeared in the *Philadelphia Inquirer* across the state. I kept my composure through it all, but I would be barred by a judge from the house for the next two and a half months.

I initially stayed at the home of Tom Murphy, the mayor of Pittsburgh, for two weeks, and then he arranged for me to move in with his elderly mother-in-law who had a spare room in her apartment. She became just like my mother for the next two months, and I couldn't have landed in better circumstances during this very trying time. Tom and I had worked together closely while I was in office and we had become very good friends. He was almost like an older brother to me. Robert Kimball, the owner of the firm that I worked for, also treated me like a son and stood by my side through the whole ordeal. During times like these you find out who your real friends are.

Eventually the Brentwood police dropped all of the charges against me because the local magistrate had the wisdom to understand what had really happened. But I had gone through a horrendous experience in the process. Unfortunately, the papers didn't bother to put the dismissal of my case on the front page as they had done with my arrest.

While I was gone from the house, things went from bad to worse with my sons. My older brother Wesley went over to the house a few weeks after the fight and told me that the place just seemed to be "evil." Bobby and Charlie were gleeful and had no remorse whatsoever as to what had happened to me. Bobby would later reveal how living in the house made him feel at that time. "You'd come in here and the atmosphere was different from outside. You could tell it was the house because you'd get outside the house and you'd be fine, but when you were interacting inside the house it was bad. No one got along, no one liked one another, it was a scary place. It influenced our lives."

During these difficult months, I seriously considered getting a divorce and not going home. Even Lesa had been defending Bobby during the fight. In retrospect I realize that surreptitiously the evil entity was working on Bobby and Charlie, and it had worked on Lesa, turning them all against me. The object of the evil at the time was to get me out of the way, to take over my family.

The next month we went to see John Arnold, the

pastor of the Baptist church that we had attended for family counseling several times. He was the same minister who had known me as a teen. He insisted that the problems were due to simple adolescent rebellion.

"I think there's something deeper going on," I told him, showing him pictures of the boys. "There's some kind of evil in my house that has affected my sons deeply. It's not just adolescent rebellion. I can feel it; there's something else going on here. They're my children. I know them."

"Bob, please calm down," he said in a patronizing tone. "Nothing has happened that can't be explained by ordinary rebellious teen behavior."

"I'm telling you that there's something much larger, of an evil spiritual nature, going on in the house," I said, trying not to raise my voice. "I'm afraid that my son Bobby may be under the influence of a demonic force. When he told me that he was going to kill me during the fight he sounded like another person, and he sounded serious. That's not the Bobby I've always known."

"Bob," he said, looking directly at me, "it's understandable that you are distraught after the fight and being barred from your home. I can imagine how painful and embarrassing that was for you. I agree that the situation got out of control. But a demonic force?" He raised his eyebrows as if he thought I was crazy.

Maybe I seemed a little crazy, but he had known me since I was a teenager and should have taken my comments more seriously. On the other hand, it was a bizarre situation and I can't blame him for being skeptical. The circumstances I was describing didn't exactly fit into the normal set of family issues he was used to dealing with.

I had a hard time attending church there after that, not only because of his attitude but because of the demeanor of the congregants. Lesa and I did not feel welcome anymore. I'd been all over the news, and these were very proper people in their "Baptist bubble" who now disapproved of me. I felt a deep despair and had no idea where to turn. What was next? How could I deal with this evil force in my house and keep my family together?

I've been asked many times why we didn't just leave the house at that point. We had tried to sell it once and failed, and now I couldn't unload it on another unsuspecting family. But there were other reasons. The haunting started off so subtly we didn't realize what was going on for a long time. The whole thing snuck up on us. Life was initially good in the house except for the crazy little things like the light in the closet and other such happenings that we'd done our best to ignore. It wasn't until everything got completely out of control that I asked myself, now what do I do? But by then it was too late. I had been expelled from the house, and both Bobby and Charlie would develop such wild, destructive, and anxiety-driven behavior that they would end up in Western Psychiatric Hospital the following year. Lesa had already been in the Allegheny General psychiatric unit. So many things exploded at the same time that I was in survival mode, dealing with one thing after another and keeping things together as best I could.

When I finally realized how much the evil presence in our house was affecting my family and our relationship,

I really didn't know whether or not it would follow us if we did leave. We had a cottage at a lake, and we had seen and experienced paranormal things there, too, during the same period. Once, when Jessica's friend woke up there during the night, she saw someone beside the bed. On other occasions things had mysteriously fallen off the wall and doors had closed by themselves.

Last but not least, it's my nature to confront a challenge head-on, to stand my ground and fight. I am not the type to back down in the face of a powerful adversary. I proved that when I went up against the political establishment in Pittsburgh. I felt prepared to face whatever this thing was and was sure that my faith would buttress my determination. Plus I once again had my wife on my side. Lesa and I both felt that battling the evil that threatened to destroy our family was something we needed to do together.

It was not long after we left Library Baptist that Lesa and I began to attend Catholic Mass at St. Sylvester Church, the local parish. I had been baptized there as a baby, served as an altar boy, and also attended the Catholic grade school there. A sense of peace and determination began to strengthen me as I realized that I could possibly seek help with our battle from the Catholic Church.

PART TWO

CHAPTER NINE

Right after I returned to the house before Christmas of 2003, things really became unhinged. The paranormal activity became more regular and much more intense, and by January the lid blew off. Again it began in the coat closet.

One day, right after Christmas, I opened the closet to get my coat. Before I got to the back door, I realized I'd forgotten my gloves. I returned to the closet and reached for the light chain. My hand encountered only empty space. With great trepidation, I slowly reached upward. Was it happening again? My fingers touched the chain and nearly recoiled as I realized it was wrapped around the top of the light, just like before. A chill and sense of dread ran through me. I'd pulled that chain less than a minute ago. Yet something had managed to rewrap it in the few seconds the door was closed. The supernatural force was now present again and again resident inside the closet.

The next day I tried an experiment. Before we went to church, I took some rosary beads that had belonged to my grandmother and tied them to the pull chain with a knot. When we returned home I found the chain with the rosaries wrapped around the light. I hung them straight again, ate lunch, and returned to find the rosary beads untied from the chain and hanging on a coat hook. The chain was wrapped back around the light. This went on as I experimented with the rosaries and other objects. I hung a small brass weight of about an ounce on the chain, and it, too, was placed on top of the light with the chain in just a few minutes after closing the door. But the one thing I did discover for certain: This thing, whatever it was, did not like rosary beads; in fact, it seemed to hate them. By the end of the day I realized that this was not a game, or if it was, it was being played in deadly earnest and I wasn't aware of the rules.

I then decided to shut myself in the closet and read the Bible aloud. As I did this I could feel the presence of something in the closet with me. My skin crawled and the same sense of dread came over me. Despite this feeling, I kept at it and read aloud from the Bible several times for about a half hour each time and found that it had no impact whatsoever on the chain-related activity. I was convinced that if this "thing" was evil I would see how it reacted to the spoken word of God. I left the light on and the door open, and I heard the chain moving as I stood a few feet away in the foyer.

At this point I knew that I had to seek out outside guidance.

I decided to turn to Mother Maria at the Passionist convent for help. I called and left a message for her and said that it was somewhat urgent. Within a few minutes she called me back.

"Mother Maria, something is going on here that's unnatural. I believe my house is occupied by some kind of supernatural force." She was well aware of what had happened with my boys, and seemed now to know what was happening in the house since I returned, including how the spirit reacted to the rosaries and my reading of the Bible. She was very calm and seemed unfazed by what I was describing so I kept talking.

"Bob, you probably don't know this," she replied when I finished, in a very matter-of-fact tone of voice, as if we were discussing the most mundane topic. "Most people aren't aware of it, but there is a phenomenon called demonic infestation. It's not that uncommon in houses where serious sins have once taken place. Evil associated with the sins can remain and torment the house and its occupants indefinitely if it isn't expelled."

I couldn't imagine what serious sins had taken place in my house. Certainly nothing since we had lived there. I now understood that our ghost might not be a ghost at all, but a full-fledged evil entity, as I wasn't ready for the word "demon" at that point. It felt unreal, like I was in a horror movie or documentary.

"How do we know this is an evil entity, Mother, and not just a ghost? I mean a lot of old houses are supposedly haunted." I knew in my heart it wasn't a ghost, but I was still looking for a less ominous explanation.

"You don't know, not yet. But the influence on your children and the dissension in your family, plus the reaction to the rosary suggests demonic activity. I think you need to contact a priest at the Passionist monastery for help. They do deliverance work."

Again, I was surprised by her matter-of-factness, but I decided to do as she said and took down the information she gave me.

The next night when I came home from work, Lesa took me to the kitchen and showed me the charred remains of what appeared to be a music CD lying on the kitchen counter. It looked like a plate shattered into many pieces. Bobby, in one of his rare moments of friendliness toward us, came in to describe what had happened.

"Dad, you're not going to believe this," he said, wide-eyed and obviously frightened. "I almost got killed by a flying CD."

He explained how a few hours earlier he and his girlfriend, Becky, had gone into his bedroom (the blue room) and as he was standing by the door he heard a loud "pop" behind him. Something had whizzed right by his head, slammed into the wall, and exploded. They looked and saw the shattered remains of the CD lying on the floor. This disc flew at him as if it had been shot out of a gun and hit the wall with such force that it left an imprint in the plaster. If it had been one inch closer to Bobby's head it might have done him serious injury. It was also a CD that had disappeared some weeks before. He thought that he had lost it.

Bobby had no idea what was going on with the chain in the closet, so I explained it to him. He may have understood more than I thought, because he undoubtedly remembered what happened in his room with the black figure when he was a child, even though he had not yet revealed it to anyone. I then took my Bible and headed for his room. I closed the door and spent about an hour reading scripture aloud and declaring that this house belonged to me. I had no idea what I was doing, how naive I was at the time, or what evil had taken place in that very room decades ago, but it felt good to be doing something. I had a lot to learn during the months to come.

Mother Maria had suggested I contact a priest at the monastery that was affiliated with the convent: St. Paul of the Cross Passionist monastery. The Passionists came to the United States in 1852 and settled in Pittsburgh at the invitation of Bishop Michael O'Connor of the Diocese of Pittsburgh. Traditionally, the Passionists were founded to live a life of prayer, poverty, penance, and solitude, and to go forth as apostolic preachers to proclaim the ignominies and glories of the cross. Through "retreats" of several days they assist followers of Jesus to focus more intently upon his sacrifice, and likewise to let his "passion" or love flow through them.

The Passionist order was founded in the 1600s in Italy by St. Paul, a devout priest who it was said the Holy Spirit raised up to help people find God in their hearts. Paul was convinced that God was found most readily in the Passion of Jesus Christ. He saw this Passion as being a powerful depiction of God's love for humankind, and at the same time our best avenue for complete union with

Him. Throughout his missionary journey in creating the Passionist order, he always carried with him a large wooden crucifix in honor of the Passion of Jesus; thus he became known as "Paul of the Cross," and a great adversary of the Evil One.

The Passionist order encourages a deeper, almost mystical religious experience and a much more personal relationship with Jesus than traditional Catholicism. Some of their priests exercise "supernatural gifts." Some are also involved in what they call deliverance work, which involves freeing those influenced or oppressed by evil forces.

So it was to these prayer warriors I was sent to seek guidance and relief from the evil that infested our home. I discovered I was sent to the right place, again, by what I believe to be divine providence.

CHAPTER TEN

Father Ed Moran had been a Passionist priest for fifty years. His white hair, beard, and jolly disposition reminded me of depictions of St. Nicholas. I had met him several times at the convent chapel and once invited him to breakfast after Mass. He had a very disarming and calming nature, and he never failed to cheer me up.

Since I'd asked him to Sunday dinner about a year earlier, I figured I knew him well enough to approach him with my situation. So I called and asked if I could stop by the monastery to talk with him.

He led me down a hallway of the old building to a small sitting room. The whole place had an overwhelming sense of peace about it. I felt as though I was in a warm, spiritual atmosphere in contrast to the chaos I was experiencing in my home. Fr. Ed had appeared at the door, a friendly, inviting smile on his face. "The Lord's blessings to you," he said, before wrapping me in a cordial hug.

"Mother Maria at the convent told me to seek the help of a priest at the Passionist monastery, and you're the only one I know," I said, after explaining the purpose of my visit.

"I hope I can help, but I'm not really an expert in deliverance work. I assume that's what you want. I'll do what I can, though."

I went on to describe what was happening with my house and my family. He already knew of the incident with my son. Everyone in western Pennsylvania knew.

"I've had some minor experience in dealing with 'infestation' cases, Bob, and I'm willing to do what I can."

I was surprised at how he reacted to my request. His eyes didn't grow wide and he didn't look at me with disbelief. He was very businesslike. It was as if I were talking to the Orkin man about having termites in the house exterminated!

"However, in some cases," Fr. Ed went on, "the demon spirits tend to be possessive of the dwelling and their expulsion can be a long, arduous process. If that's the case here there's another priest at the monastery who has much more experience than me, and we can ask him to get involved as well."

I hoped that it wouldn't be a long process, but from what I had experienced so far, I suspected that it would be. We agreed that he would come to the house that weekend and celebrate Mass with the family and then pray prayers of expulsion. This all hearkened back to when we had bought the house and Mr. McHenry told me that they had once had Mass in the living room. I now knew why, and the many pieces of a large puzzle were just starting to fall into place.

Fr. Ed came on a Saturday evening in late January. By now, everyone in the family knew that we were facing something supernatural, and even Bobby agreed to participate. He insisted that his girlfriend attend as well, because they were inseparable at the time, and she was the one who had seen the CD fly across the room. Becky dressed in the same all-black Goth manner as he and rarely said a word. Even though she was a very attractive little girl, her black clothes, black makeup, and contrasting white complexion could have landed her a spot in the movie *The Addams Family*. Charlie and David were present as well, but Jessica and Collin were only there at the beginning and then they left. Jessica thought that Collin would be a distraction and was a little wary of the ceremony to begin with. They were not living in the house at that point, because during my banishment she had moved in with her new fiancé, Tom, and his family. The tension in the house with the boys had become too much for her, and she wanted Collin away from the turmoil.

I made a fire in the fireplace and tried to create as calm an atmosphere as I could. We were sitting in an impressive space. The living room measures twenty-three by fifteen feet with nine-foot ceilings. The fireplace front is nine feet wide and made of classic Roman brick, with a large mantel supported by four large carved ornamental braces. The five-foot entrance to the room is closed in by two large oak pocket doors. It was a very fitting setting for a prayer service, as I'm sure it had been for the McHenrys as well.

Fr. Ed began by explaining in general terms how and why spirits can occupy a house and what we would be doing that evening.

"Please don't be frightened," he reassured us. "I believe the power of God can banish evil spirits. I'm here to help cleanse your home of evil so that it will leave and never return."

He then went on to celebrate Mass and administer the sacrament of the Eucharist to all of us. Even though my sons were not baptized Catholic, they had attended the local Catholic grade school and attended Mass many times with my mother. They were very familiar with Catholic ritual. After the Mass, Fr. Ed went through a long series of prayers for the family and the house, asking for peace to dwell in us and it, and that any unsettled or evil spirits should depart. It was all pretty basic and paled in comparison to the extensive ceremonies and blessings we would go through during the coming two years that would sometimes take hours to perform. But at this point this ceremony certainly seemed adequate, and all was happy and peaceful when I took Fr. Ed back to the monastery.

Little did I know that we had only fired a first shot in a battle that would continue to escalate into pitched warfare over the next two years. I was still under the impression that this evening could be the quick fix I hoped for. I couldn't have been more wrong.

The next day I awoke to find all of my art collection hanging cockeyed on the walls throughout the first floor—nine pictures in three rooms. I collect the classic early American artwork of Robert Griffing. He has become a friend over the years, and the house is filled with his various lithograph prints under glass, large reproductions on canvas, and one cherished original he painted specifically for me. They are all eastern American Indian scenes, most having to do with war, which is a strange coincidence considering the crimes I eventually discovered that were committed by Native Americans on the ground the house is built on. My attraction to these Native American scenes interestingly began right after we moved in.

Apparently the evil entity wasn't a fan of my prized collection, or perhaps was trying to send me a message. With a few exceptions, during these early days of the struggle the entity's activity mostly consisted of nuisance tactics intended to unsettle us. It would move furniture and pictures, and it once turned the water on in the third-floor bathroom while plugging the sink so that the water eventually made its way down to the first floor. We weren't home when it happened and came back to find the mess. Another time I had started a slow-running hot bath, calculating that it would take about ten minutes for the tub to fill up. This was my nightly ritual for years. On this night I went into another room to finish writing what had happened that day in my journal only to hear Lesa screaming to me just a couple of minutes later that there was water coming down into the kitchen, which was below our bathroom. I ran to the tub to find both the cold and hot water handles wide open and the tub overflowing! I could almost hear the thing laughing at me.

These old houses are built strong, and the water did no damage on either occasion. We dried up the mess and moved on. The damage was more likely to be done to us. The evil entity apparently would derive energy from discord within the family and had done so for years. When we would fight with one another it would become stronger, and it was able to manipulate our tempers in ways that would send us off at one another in an instant. Throughout the years I would fly into a rage for any reason. Lesa's increasing proclivity to spend money I felt that we didn't have would send me off the deep end regularly. The boys fought with one another from the time that they could walk, and when we got drawn into their battles it just added to the turmoil.

Another thing I would learn as the months progressed was that the spirit would always react to positive steps that we took against it. When we would push, it would push back. When we would have Mass in the house it would create havoc for a few days and then things would settle down, but it was always lurking. Pictures were moved or knocked off the wall, clocks and watches stopped, electric devices such as the coffeemaker and toaster wouldn't work, plugs were pulled out of outlets, and the computer was constantly going haywire. Every day in the basement I found that the lights and radio were on, and the chair was pulled up in front of the woodstove just like it had been during our first years in the house.

And so began the process of poking and jabbing at this thing in an attempt to make its existence as miserable as it had made ours. The question was, how to do it? A struggle is only ended when the two sides battle each other long enough so that one side relents and gives up. I knew we had to stick with it—this was the only path to an eventual victory.

I had much to learn about fighting this battle. Over time I began to see a pattern. This thing would expend energy to manifest itself for a period of time in dramatic ways and then it would withdraw. It would eventually possess rooms with its stench, create puddles of blood-like fluid on the floors, scratch and bite us at night while we slept, and give us wild, terrifying nightmares, just to give a few examples. It seemed to me that it would use energy to perform these acts in an attempt to terrify us and then it would have to retreat to build up strength. This pattern went on for some time until its manifestations became more intense and occurred almost on a daily basis, but by then we had learned how to confront it continuously as well. As we learned to live with these events, and almost treated them as routine, then it would up the stakes and devise some new terror tactic.

Even after that terrible fight with the boys, Lesa still trusted my judgment and said that she was prepared to follow my lead and see this confrontation through. The spirit had played havoc with her mind over the years and had done its best to break up our marriage. But now that it was focused on the boys, her motherly instincts wanted to fight back as much as I did, so we strengthened our determination to fight it together. Neither of us has ever regretted that decision.

Fr. Ed called periodically to ask how things were going.

"Things haven't improved, Father. In fact they've gotten worse since your visit. What do you think is going on here? Shouldn't things have gotten better after you celebrated Mass in the house?"

"You need to keep things as peaceful as possible within the family, Bob. That's crucial to getting rid of this thing," Fr. Ed advised in his usual calm and kindly tone.

"But the boys are getting progressively worse, Father. That's what really worries me the most." I was frustrated, and I'm sure my voice reflected that.

"Have you sought help for them, Bobby in particular? Even if there's a supernatural influence, sometimes a therapist can do a world of good. Or maybe medication?"

"Yes, we have. We've taken every step and they're seeing psychiatrists, Father, but it doesn't seem to be working. This thing is focusing on the boys. They're the most vulnerable. This house is progressively becoming a literal Hell to live in. Not only are the boys angry and rebellious, but they're becoming suicidal. Plus every day the thing lets us know it's here by playing some new stupid prank—either flooding the bathroom, making pounding noises, moving furniture, shorting out electrical appliances. I believe that it's attempting to wear me and Lesa down psychologically. I can feel it."

Several weeks into February, as things were looking grim, Fr. Ed told me that he had talked with the other priest at the monastery who had more experience with these matters. His name was Fr. Mike Salvagna, and even though he was not an official exorcist of the church, he had a somewhat unofficial deliverance ministry that had gained him a reputation. When people called the Diocese of Pittsburgh for help they would be referred to him. He agreed to come to the house and meet with us along with Fr. Ed to review the case and to see if he could be of assistance. We scheduled a date in late February 2004 for both of them to visit, and I gained some strength from knowing there were reinforcements on the way. The stakes were going up, and the battle was about to intensify.

The two priests first came on a Friday night about 6:30 P.M. It was dark and cold outside, and we were happy to see them pull in the driveway. Fr. Mike is about fifteen years younger than Fr. Ed. When he got out of the car and came into the house I was a surprised to see this short, balding, unassuming priest with a warm personality. He wasn't the least bit pompous or "priestly." He greeted us with a handshake, and his sincerity and concern were immediately apparent. He looked as though he could play the role of a medieval monk in an old movie of *Robin Hood*. We went right to the living room and began to get acquainted. Both priests came dressed for the occasion and looked as though they were ready to celebrate Mass in a church. Just as I did during the first Mass, I set up an altar on a marble-topped table in the living room and gathered everything else that was required. Being an altar boy taught me well. I neatly covered the table with a white sheet that draped down to the floor. I placed two candles and a free-standing crucifix on the altar. I had a large Catholic Bible that had belonged to my mother, and a crystal oil and vinegar set on a matching tray that I filled with water and wine. Fr. Mike brought his own chalice and communion hosts. I had provided these during the first Mass with a stemmed crystal glass and round pieces of bread that I had cut and compressed flat into hosts. I also had a bell that I could ring during the consecration portion of the Mass. We were officially ready.

It would later get to a point where this altar would stand in the living room always prepared for Mass. We wouldn't dismantle it, just move it off to the side of the room because it was used so often. On many occasions we would carry it up the steps to the various rooms of the house where Mass would be celebrated, and eventually would take it to the basement. We had Mass so frequently in the house I once said jokingly to Fr. Mike that we could put a sign up out front.

Fr. Mike took quite a bit of time that first evening getting to know us. It was apparent that this priest was all business and he fully understood the situation he had been thrust into. He told us that the demon's strength would determine how long it would take to be expelled. He added that sometimes they just don't leave. This is where I disagreed with him. It was my feeling that evil can always ultimately be prevailed upon to retreat by wielding the power of Jesus, and his cross. I was convinced of it and was willing to engage it for as long as it took. He agreed, but left me with the impression that again, there wouldn't be a quick resolution.

We then celebrated Mass, and as I recall we each took a part in one of the scripture readings. Lesa and the boys participated as well as my friend Kerry Fraas. Kerry was only there to give us moral support—and because he was more than a little fascinated with the whole situation. As a devout Presbyterian, he had the standard Protestant suspicion of the Catholic Church and its priests. But he'd gotten to know my boys well when they were younger, and they looked upon him as their funny uncle, almost like John Candy of *Uncle Buck* fame.

Kerry is a big, powerfully built, handsome guy with a personality as outsized as his body, and a joker's sense of humor. The first time he came to the house after I told him what was happening he immediately broke into a perfect Bill Murray routine from the movie *Ghostbusters*. "We came, we saw, we kicked its ass!" He also did a great Dr. Evil from *Austin Powers*. With his little finger at the corner of his mouth he said, "Are you saying that this is an *evil* house?" It was pretty funny, but I'd lost my sense of humor when it came to the house. I knew by then that this was no joking matter. I'm not certain that he bought into what we were doing at that point, or if he even believed what we claimed was happening, but over the coming months Kerry became a fixture at many of the deliverance sessions and eventually came to experience, and understand, that the whole thing was in fact very real. His joking around soon stopped, as he realized that this was a deadly serious matter. I'll never forget the epiphany he had one evening as we were preparing for a deliverance session. We were sitting on the front porch when I brought down a rosary whose crucifix had recently been literally mangled by the demon. As I passed it to Kerry he held the crucifix in his right hand and the beads in his left. Just as he was examining the damage, all of a sudden the crucifix detached itself from the prayer beads, which fell and hit his wrist. I wasn't too surprised because I knew how the demon detested rosary beads. But Kerry's eyes literally bulged and he said: "You know this is real, it's really happening. And if it is real, the Devil is real, angels are real, Jesus is real, all of it is just as it is laid out in the Bible, it is all true!"

I'd been so caught up in this situation that I'd lost perspective and stopped seeing what it all really meant. "You know, Kerry, you're right," I responded, realizing that his fresh outlook was inspiring.

With his legal mind he delved into all of the books that he could find related to the subject and for a short time even became an associate of Fr. Mike in his deliverance ministry.

That night we spent a long evening going through the ceremony. It involved not only Mass and deliverance prayers but we went through the entire house with blessed candles as Fr. Mike blessed each room with holy water, from the third floor to the basement, including the crawl spaces in the attic. By then the boys had left, but Lesa and I accompanied Fr. Mike and Kerry, as Fr. Ed stayed on the first floor and prayed:

Jesus Christ come against you, with the power of God, with the angels and saints behind us, we command you in the name of Jesus Christ to leave these premises, you have no rights or authority here, this house belongs to God, it is sanctified by prayer, by the celebration of Mass, by the holiness of the people here. By the power of God we cast you into the darkness where you belong, never to return. We thank you Lord for the angels and saints who guide us and protect us and place them at the doors and windows of this house, command them to stand guard there and keep evil out, not allow evil to come in. You have given this house to the Cranmer family, it belongs to them, not to the Evil one. We claim that same blessing for every inch of this household.

You have no right or authority to be here. We break curses and spells going back to previous owners, we unbind that, unleash that, we set it free. Jesus we pray for your presence that your light may cast out the darkness. We bind and reject the fear that Satan has created in this household.

By the end of the evening we were worn out but we seemed to have run through the entire process, and I felt satisfied that we had made a significant impact. We would now wait to see what happened. However, by the next day and throughout the coming weeks our enemy would mount a counterattack that would leave us all shell-shocked.

CHAPTER ELEVEN

During February and March, Bobby would vary in moods between reserved solitude and wild tirades and rants, and we never knew when one of his volcanic eruptions would explode.

The regular harassment from the demon continued on a daily basis as well, and we did our best to put up with it. Pictures were moved, especially in our bedroom, one of our wedding and another of Bobby and Charlie in their football uniforms. This particular football picture was pulled down on almost a daily basis. I would replace it and come back upstairs later and it would be taken down again. I'd find our wedding picture hanging sideways or lying facedown on the floor or dresser.

We were always on the lookout to discover if the boys had some part in any of this activity, but that was relatively easy to rule out because it usually occurred when they weren't home. I couldn't let it go, however. I would go to great lengths questioning everyone to come up with plausible explanations as to how something out of place got that way. But activity perpetrated by the spirit usually left no doubt that it was paranormal. For instance when a clock would stop you could remove the battery and put it back in and it would start running again. This held true for watches and the pendulum in the grandfather clock as well. Lesa finally quit setting the coffeepot to start brewing automatically in the morning because it would never turn on. We bought a new coffeemaker and that one wouldn't work, either. We had to keep two alarm clocks running in our bedroom because we never knew which one wasn't going to go off in the morning. Lesa would continually find her iron turned on. Once it was set facedown and burned the cover black. After that she would unplug it and set it aside to make sure it didn't start a fire. Our two computers were always having problems as well. Anything electronic was vulnerable to malfunctions.

The spirit had its usual attraction to the furnace room in the basement, and its activity there stepped up considerably. As before, in the mornings during the winter I would go downstairs and all of the lights would be on with the radio playing. And as always the chair was positioned directly in front of the loading door for the stove. I'd put the chair back at the workbench only to find it moved again the next morning.

The kids had always said that they were scared of the basement and would run up the steps because they felt like something was chasing them. In those early years I would go out of my way to discount anything they said that related to ghostly activity. I suppose I was in denial. On some level I must have felt that if I ignored it, it wasn't real. This attitude was easier than facing the unknown.

Because of Bobby's increasingly self-destructive and aggressive behavior, Lesa had to quit her job at the University of Pittsburgh. She actually was on the verge of being fired anyway, as she was the secretary to the dean of the School of Public Health and her boss didn't quite understand our family issues, especially when Bobby was in and out of psychiatric treatment. With Lesa at home full-time again, I could at least concentrate on my own professional responsibilities.

The firm I worked for treated me very well. I considered the president of the company, the owner's son, a friend. One day I took a big chance and explained to him what we were going through with the house. Thanks to my own reputation and our close working relationship he knew that I wasn't nuts. In fact, the situation at the house actually caused me to throw myself into my work even more because it helped me forget what I would have to face when I went home. He would ask me periodically how things were going. Usually I'd just say, "It's insane," but I never discussed it unless he brought it up. I actually dreaded leaving my office and going home at night to face what was going on with my family and the house. I can recall the "stench" of the thing being present in my nostrils even at work, and it would sicken me.

Bobby was becoming extremely difficult to handle. I was frightened of him and for Lesa. We had enrolled him in a special one-on-one tutoring program, so he was at least going to school again. Getting him there, however, wasn't always easy. One morning he knocked Lesa to the floor while she was trying to get him out of bed, twisting her wrist and almost breaking her ankle. On another occasion he punched the dashboard in her car, breaking the knobs on the radio. Yet another time he punched the fender and put such a good-sized dent in it that he had to have his hand bandaged up at the emergency room.

I called the police on him twice, more to have a record of the situation than for help. Even though the assault charges against me from the previous year had been dropped, I wanted them to know what we were still dealing with, just in case I ever had to subdue him again. Thankfully the police now seemed to be on my side, knowing what I was going through with Bobby.

During these months, Fr. Mike was the biggest help to us. He would drive out to the house and meet with Bobby and talk with him while at the same time attempting to discern how deep the spiritual oppression went into his mind. He'd talk about his behavior, his clothes, his music, and his thoughts of his family. And as one might expect, those thoughts weren't pretty. He also did this to see if Bobby was at a point where he would do serious harm to himself, or us. At one time he thought that it would be beneficial if we took him to the monastery where he could be counseled more thoroughly. Kerry and I drove Bobby to meet with Fr. Mike at the monastery one Sunday afternoon.

We went into a small sitting room that had been prepared, and we sat down with Fr. Mike directly in front of Bobby. After some general prayers, Fr. Mike began to ask Bobby about what remained of his faith and specifically of the sacrificial death of Jesus on the cross. He had to reply with very direct answers that, as I understood, he would not have been able to give if the demon had a grip on him, or if, in fact, he was possessed. He answered all of the questions and became very calm and docile, and I saw a glimpse of the Bobby I knew before the wild behavior, black clothes, and black music took over his life. Why didn't I banish all of this stuff from the house? I knew it would just make a bad situation much worse. He had to get to the point where he would get rid of it voluntarily, and we were far more concerned with his own fragile state of mind. He had been diagnosed as being bipolar and was in counseling and on medication. But his problems went way beyond psychological disturbance, crossing the line into demonic oppression.

Fr. Mike later explained to us the levels of demonic oppression and possession.

"The name of Jesus is one big red flag," he said. "Possessed people can't say or respond to things of a spiritual nature. I worked with a woman whom eight different priests tried to help—you couldn't say the name of Jesus in front of her—luckily Bobby was nowhere near that. There are levels of demonic oppression. When it becomes obsessive that means the Evil One is intruding more strongly."

Bobby's issues seemed to have started from the first

day we moved into the house; his room obviously was an issue. The evil was strongest there, and it focused its attention on him, just as it shifted to Lesa when we moved into the blue room. When he subsequently moved back into the blue room he changed dramatically.

Fr. Mike went on to explain Satan's ultimate objective. "Ultimately he wants to kill us. A chain is as strong as its weakest link. In your family, that weak link is Bobby, and the evil has manifested itself in violence and rebellion. It's like a hand and a glove. The hand represents the weaknesses that are there in the first place, then suddenly you put an evil glove on that hand and you're in real trouble. The glove tries to keep that evil inside the person. In order to get free we need to get rid of the glove. That's what the prayers do. At the same time Christian living is very important. People ultimately have to freely manifest their discipleship in Jesus, and attempt to follow his example in life. The objective of the Evil One is obviously the exact opposite, he seeks to hurt, kill, and destroy."

Fr. Mike was not always available each time I felt that a Mass was required in the house during the spring and summer of 2004. Fr. Ed, however, was generally always there to accommodate us. But I noticed that his health was declining and his sight was worsening. He was also involved in a serious car crash. I knew that demons have a way of reaching out to attack the priests involved, and I didn't want my house to be the cause of this holy man's demise. Things in the house weren't getting any better, but I knew that the entity hated Mass to be celebrated, so I wanted to keep striking at it. The regular Masses were in fact making the situation much worse, or more intense, but Fr. Ed appeared to be paying a price, and I didn't want to put him at further risk.

By 2003, Jessica was in college and had found a young guy named Tom with whom she fell in love, and she and Collin had moved in with him and his family. She asked if they could move back in with us on the third floor so they could save money. I thought that their presence might settle the boys down. Also, Jessica was always the least affected by the entity—or so I thought at the time. I certainly wanted the best for her, but I said that the only way I would permit them to move into the house would be if she and Tom were married. With this decision we were soon in the throes of planning a wedding.

Jessica and Tom were married in May 2004. The wedding was a grand affair, and they soon prepared to move into their new home. I was concerned at the time because the activity in the house had started to become even more intense, but it seemed to be confined to certain areas of the first and second floors.

There was a brief respite in the weeks prior to the wedding while we had new carpet installed on the second and third floors. I was happy to have this distraction but wasn't sure how things would go after they moved in. Bobby was friendly with my new son-in-law, and I hoped that Tom's strong personality and maturity would help him. Bobby was still exhibiting extremely violent behavior toward Lesa and me, to the point that the police continued to be involved on several occasions, while

Charlie was continuing to experience extreme fits of anxiety that totally incapacitated him at times. But the wedding brought peace and some composure to our family, and things settled down for a while.

The day came when the new young family was to move into the house and all of the preparations were made to turn the third floor into their home. A room on the third floor that sits apart from the living area, and had traditionally been used as an attic storage room, was cleaned out, painted a light blue with yellow flowers, and converted into a bedroom for Collin. To be on the safe side I asked Fr. Ed to conduct a ritual blessing of the third floor the weekend that they moved in when they got back from their honeymoon. All went well and I believed that the third floor was protected. I also had confidence that the paranormal activity in the house in general would soon be under control as well, as it had lessened recently. I was not prepared to give an inch to this thing and was determined to use the house as I intended—as our home!

Later that night my son-in-law was walking up the steps and stopped to look in on Collin, who had been put to bed about an hour earlier. The room was dark, but light was shining in the window from the moon outside. To his surprise he saw the back of a figure standing at the bed bent over the sleeping little boy. Naturally thinking that it was Jessica he said, "What are you doing in here with the light off?" When the figure did not turn around but moved into the wall that led to a crawl space and disappeared, Tom followed quickly to see who it was and then stood there mystified beside the bed wondering what he had just seen. He picked up Collin and went into the apartment where Jessica was watching television. Speaking excitedly he told her what had just happened, expressing complete befuddlement. Up to this point the problems with the house had been kept as a family secret, except for the priests involved with a few others in confidence, and Jessica had never told her new husband any of the stories. If she had, he would not have believed her anyway. And since she had moved out of the house before the newer intense activity had begun, she hadn't experienced anything recently.

She then called me upstairs with Lesa.

"Tom, tell my dad what you just saw."

"I saw this black figure bending over Collin's bed. Then it faded into the wall. What the Hell?"

"Well, that's a way to put it," I said, joking weakly. "Tom, this is really hard to explain," I tried to sound reassuring, "and you might not believe it, but we have some type of presence in this house." I realized as I said it how unbelievable and crazy it sounded.

"You have to be kidding. You mean a ghost?"

"Kind of a ghost," I responded, "but a lot worse. Ghosts are usually just spirits of people who died in the house. This thing is different." Again, I tried to sound matter-of-fact, but I saw the expression on his face. He didn't want to believe me. It all sounded too bizarre. But then he couldn't understand what he had seen; the figure just moved into the wall and disappeared!

"You need to keep Collin in bed with you for the night and we'll deal with it in the morning." Tom was more than agreeable. Despite his skepticism, the incident had obviously shaken him.

I had done my best to be calm, cool, and collected, but when Lesa and I went downstairs I realized I was more shaken than them, even though I had tried not to show it. This incident told me that our situation was not getting any better; it was getting dangerously worse. Opposite to my expectations, the activity had moved to the third floor and was now targeting the baby. I was angry and mystified as to what I was going to do in the face of this new escalation. Now that I had more "innocents" to worry about, how would I protect them? Had the thing been doing this all along when Jessica was initially living with us? Was it hurting the baby and in some way responsible for his developmental issues? A thousand thoughts streamed through my mind. What was I to do? This thing was openly threatening the most innocent member of the family now. I had to do something soon; I just didn't know what. Jessica and Tom couldn't afford their own place, and Jessica wanted to live with us in the house until they could.

The baby continued to sleep with Jessica in her bed for the rest of the week. The strange event in Collin's bedroom was shocking, and I called the priests in. They were scheduled to return the next week. Jessica's husband was planning to go fishing with his friends that weekend. He left the following Saturday morning. Nothing out of the ordinary took place during the week, and the significance of the event began to fade.

That Saturday night I went to bed before Lesa, who was reading a book down in the kitchen. Sometime after midnight, Jessica called on her cell phone to her mother downstairs, screaming incoherently. Lesa ran upstairs to the third floor without ever stopping to wake me in the second-floor bedroom.

"Mom, I was so scared," Jessica was sobbing, sitting up straight in bed. Collin was awake but surprisingly calm.

"Why, what happened?" Lesa, who was shaking by this point, reached out to hold her.

"Me and Collin were sleeping when I woke up to see this thing all in black standing at the foot of my bed." Jessica turned and pointed to the streetlight. The light was streaming in, illuminating the room. "I could see this hideously grotesque face smiling at me. I can't tell you how horrible it was. I couldn't move my arms or legs—it was as if they were being held down by some type of force. I got out a little scream and it finally moved out of the room right through the door. I remember this used to happen to me when I first moved up here when I was thirteen. I'd wake up and couldn't move. Now, after seeing that thing I know what was happening, it was here then, too, it all makes sense."

We were just hearing about this. Jessica had never told us about her episodes of sleep paralysis as a teenager because she really didn't know what was happening at the time and thought that she might be dreaming. Now, after this frightening episode, what actually caused it became very clear to her.

"I'll stay in here with you both tonight," Lesa said. By this time, it was so late that she never bothered to wake me. She told me what had happened the next morning when she came downstairs to get me up for church.

When we came home later that day after church we discovered the door to the bathroom that adjoins our bedroom was locked. The door has no external locking mechanism, only a lock that worked with an old skeleton key that we kept in a jewelry box on a dresser, so we knew that this was just more of the same harassment. From that point on doors would lock us in and out of rooms on a regular basis, and on one occasion, when Lesa came back from the grocery store, the front and back doors locked as I sat reading in the library. She complained and asked me why I had locked her out in the middle of the day. These types of events became almost routine to us, and we learned to live with them. We just wondered what this thing would come up with next.

Since the priests were not coming back until the following week I decided that I had to take some action. Starting on Monday night I planned to spend the evening in Collin's bedroom reading scripture and praying off and on throughout the night. I was going to push back and see what happened. Collin was still sleeping with Jessica and Tom directly across the hall in the apartment area, which consisted of a bedroom and sitting area, a living room, a kitchen, and a full bathroom.

The night I picked to begin this vigil could have been right out of a horror movie. It was the proverbial "dark and stormy night" with rain coming down hard and pounding on the windows, complete with lightning and cracking thunder. I had once used the room Collin now slept in as an office, as it was a perfect place to be tucked away completely secluded from the rest of the house to read books undisturbed or to write. Tonight it just seemed very isolated.

The room is actually a very large dormer with slanted ceilings and a large chimney, which rises through its center and divides it into two equal sections large enough for a walkway and a twin bed on each side. On the far end of the room are the windows, a large standard one in the center and two tall vertical hinged windows on either side. In front of the windows there was a stuffed chair and a lamp stand. I began the night reading various chapters of the New Testament out loud as prayers that talk about the power of the blood of Jesus and His sacrificial death for the sins of mankind. I also read Isaiah chapter 53, from the Old Testament which details the crucifixion. I understood this to be the most unbearable words for evil spirits to hear spoken aloud. Fr. Mike had told me that it apparently drives them crazy, and I was more than happy to accommodate. I continued with similar prayers until well after midnight and eventually lay down on a cot and began to pray the rosary. Knowing that I would probably doze off, I set an alarm clock for 2:00 A.M. When it went off I awoke to find that the rosary beads were missing. I found them on the floor and discovered that the links had been pushed together in a series of four figure eights. The links were not bent or broken, but were perfectly linked together as if a jeweler had done it. Of course this was physically impossible and I couldn't figure it out. I stared at the rosary, hardly believing my eyes. They were crystal beads that had been given to my deceased mother as a gift and came from Medjugorje, the famous site in Bosnia and Herzegovina where it is said messages were received from the Blessed Mother Mary. In the coming months this would become a nightly occurrence with any rosary beads I prayed with as I fell off to sleep.

It was a very tedious process to take these beads apart, because the links would be connected to one another without being opened. Since I had no magical powers, each day I would disconnect them with some miniature needle-nose pliers. In time I learned to do this quite efficiently. Sometimes they would only be interconnected in two or three places; other times as many as six linked circles would be formed. I was told by Fr. Mike that the entity did this to prevent me from praying the rosary, that it absolutely despised the rosary. Later on I would eventually come to use a large black set of beads similar to the ones I remembered the nuns would carry when I was in grade school. The spirit seemed to leave these beads alone, and they were only interconnected on a few occasions while all others were interconnected like toys every day. (I still sleep with those black rosary beads to this day.) That night, after I discovered the connected rosary beads, I got up and went back to the chair and began once again to read aloud from the Bible.

By this time the thunderstorm outside was really raging. I heard loud claps of thunder and saw bursts of lightning through the large dormer windows. It all seemed too eerie, almost staged, but I took it as a challenge and gained strength from the scriptures I was reading about the "power in the blood." I felt that I had the power in my hands and in my voice now. I would not be afraid of this thing or back down, as I wanted to put a stick in its eye!

"In whom we have redemption through His blood, the forgiveness of sin, according to the riches of His grace," I boldly proclaimed.

I went on reciting verses from Ephesians, Isaiah, Colossians, and Philippians. "That at the name of Jesus every knee should bow!"

When I got drowsy I set the alarm for 3:30 A.M. and went back to the cot and fell asleep. I was then startled awake by a loud pounding on the wall directly behind my head coming from the crawl space. This area was behind the wall and was also used for storage through a small access door. As I got up I continued to hear some movement in the space. I removed a door into the area and once again began to read the Bible aloud in a very strong voice. I believed that I was getting to the thing and would simply keep poking at it. You'd think that I would have been terrified at this point, and to be truthful a part of me was, but I drew such strength from the words that I was reading that it seemed as if I were firing a spiritual machine gun into that crawl space. But truly I didn't know what was going to happen next, and I was flying by the seat of my pants.

This went on for some time, with the rain and thunder continuing unabated. I eventually put the panel back in place and lay back down, refusing to retreat from the room. I was exhausted and fell asleep once again. The next time I awoke it was almost daylight and I immediately felt an irritation on the right side of my neck. I probed the area with my finger and it hurt. I then went downstairs to the bathroom in our bedroom and looked in the mirror to see three long, deep scratches on my neck that started below my right ear and continued down my neck underneath the shirt I was wearing—which was buttoned. These three scratches were very pronounced and looked like a cat had clawed me. There was no blood, but the area was red and inflamed. I went to bed and slept for an hour or so until it was time to get up for work.

I showed Lesa the scratches in the morning, and she responded with disbelief. She couldn't know that she'd eventually experience similar wounds of her own. Later that day, as I was at the gym working out, I could see the scratches protruding, and with physical exertion they became even more pronounced. I was somewhat alarmed but figured I had gotten to it. What would do next? I told myself that as long as I faced the presence through the power of the cross I would be protected from serious harm. At least I hoped I would!

I went on to spend the next three nights in the room, working through the same process minus the rain, lightning, and thunder. There were no more scratches over those three nights, and compared to the first night they were rather uneventful. In fact it became somewhat peaceful in there. I did, however, place a radio in the crawl space set to the local religious radio station that played during the day. Those familiar with J. Vernon McGee and his show *Thru the Bible* know he'd cause any demon to flee!

During those three days Lesa heard rumblings and the sounds of moving furniture coming from the second floor a number of times when she was in the house alone. She called me at work, and I told her not to worry about it, to simply ignore it and pray. Things settled down by the end of the week, and we felt confident that we would push back hard the following week when Fr. Mike came to the house. I had experienced what this thing didn't like and was determined to give it more of the same. I now felt a little empowered.

War was what this enemy had started, and I planned to give it all that it could take. But as it turned out, the battle was just beginning. This thing was much stronger than I suspected, and it was preparing to give us the fight of our lives.

CHAPTER TWELVE

By this time, the battle had lasted many months, and there seemed to be no sign of it subsiding. The demon was as active as ever, but thankfully Bobby had settled down quite a bit. Or maybe I was just so used to his outbursts that they didn't upset me as much. During one meltdown he'd punched his right hand completely through a plaster wall, lath boards and all. I just cleaned it up matter-of-factly, relieved that he hadn't hit the wall near a stud, because he would have shattered his hand.

Sometime in early June I had occasion to talk with my friend Tom Murphy, the mayor of Pittsburgh, and he asked me how things were going with the house. I told him that things had not improved and I really didn't know where they were headed. That we were simply dealing with it day to day, and that it felt like trench warfare, a daily murderous grind with no end in sight. He took it upon himself to make a suggestion. "Let me call the bishop." As the mayor he could pick up the phone and call him without having to give a reason, whereas anyone else would have to go through a series of gatekeepers. I knew Bishop Wuerl (now Cardinal Wuerl, archbishop of Washington D.C.) from when I was a commissioner, and I had been to his home on a number of occasions. I never thought of going to him directly, so I told Tom to go ahead and call him.

Fr. Mike was concerned as to what the response would be, because he was way down in the hierarchy of the diocese from the bishop and I had the impression he felt that his deliverance ministry, even though it did have diocesan approval, was viewed as a "wildcat operation." He was worried that he might be taken off the case. He had invested a lot of time and had developed a sincere attachment and concern for me and my family. I understood his anxiety.

The bishop's response was initially disappointing. He told Tom there was little formal experience in the diocese concerning such matters but he'd get back to us after it was discussed internally. We already knew that referrals were directed to the Passionist monastery, to Fr. Mike, and that's where we already were. This wasn't news to me. I figured that we'd have to continue to blaze this trail on our own. Fr. Mike, probably knowing that the diocese had little expertise to draw upon, was hoping our case would finally lead to a formal recognition of his ministry. He was looking for acknowledgment that more emphasis and attention should be directed to these situations, that external evil forces really did plague ordinary people.

But to my surprise, about a week later Tom called me back and told me that he had been contacted by someone who worked with the bishop. He gave me a phone number and the name of a priest that I was to call that evening at 7:00 P.M., who was prepared to get involved with my case. I'm not certain what conversations took place, but I now know that the bishop had granted me access to a formidable weapon in the realm of spiritual warfare.

Fr. Ron Lengwin was the bishop's right-hand man. He was the spokesman and community representative for the diocese, and has since become the vicar general. For years he has been the face of the Pittsburgh Diocese and is known throughout the U.S. Catholic Church. Since 1978 he has hosted a weekly two-hour radio show on Sunday nights called *Amplify*, which is broadcast from KDKA radio in Pittsburgh and reaches thirty-eight states and half of Canada (streaming online now as well). I thought initially that he would further direct me to other church experts, as he was representing the bishop. But to my surprise he ended up being our "go-to guy."

I had met Fr. Ron several times in the past when I was a commissioner. He'd always come across as being very formal and a somewhat "corporate Catholic," with rather traditional, conservative views, so I couldn't imagine him getting personally involved in our case. Nonetheless, I called him at the assigned hour of 7:00 P.M. that evening and he got right to the point. He told me that he had been assigned by the bishop to work on the case. I took solace and relief from his statement but wondered what this really meant. I had had visions of the bishop decked out in his full regalia with his tall hat and staff in hand coming to the house to expel this thing, but soon learned that wasn't about to happen. The bishop would be kept "informed," I was told.

Fr. Ron had his usual businesslike demeanor and was thoroughly prepared for our talk. My sanity was in no way questioned, and we discussed my situation as if it were a serious medical condition, not unlike a conversation with a doctor concerning a disease.

What I didn't know until much later, while preparing to write this book, was that Fr. Ron had at his disposal a remarkable Catholic "intuitive" named Connie Valenti, a longtime friend of his and known to the bishop. She is a very religious Christian woman who wanted no publicity even though she did once help the police with a serious investigation. Connie is in her late seventies and had a few negative experiences long before the paranormal craze was in vogue. Some had declared her to be a witch, at a time when people with her abilities and talents were considered unnatural or even "evil." From that point on she'd avoided notoriety. She viewed her gifts as coming from God and thus guarded them as such. She'd led a very private life for forty years and had never been called upon to deal with a case like ours. However, when asked by Fr. Ron to get involved she was willing to share her extraordinary visions with him to help unravel the mysteries of our house.

Fr. Ron never came to the house—in fact he has never been to my house to this day—and never told me he was working with anyone. It seems Connie had advised him not to come to my house, both because she was afraid for his safety and because she didn't want her visions to be affected in any way by what he would have seen if he'd visited. She'd give him a series of questions to ask me that related to her visions of the house. When I asked him a question he'd often say, "Let me get back to you on that," so he could confer with Connie, and I had no idea of her involvement. Over the course of his involvement in our situation, we generally only spoke on the phone. This later created some problems with Fr. Mike, who couldn't understand why Fr. Ron wouldn't come to the house and help with the prayer and cleansing rituals.

"Has there been a lot of turmoil and spiritual activity in one particular room on the second floor?" Fr. Ron asked me. "This room is at the top of the steps and to the left."

"Yes, there has." I was stunned. How could he know this? "It's my son's room." I told him we had sensed a problem with it going back to the initial blessing of the house in 1988 when Bobby wouldn't let the priest enter it.

"You need to go out right now and buy gold crosses for everyone in the family to wear around their necks."

"OK," I told him. I'd buy them the next day, no problem.

"Also, buy a new container of salt and go through the house room by room, throwing a small pinch of the salt in every corner, including the entrances. As you do this repeat, 'You are to leave this house, leave my family alone, and go back to where you came from.' After you're finished, dispose of the rest of the salt somewhere away from the property."

That sounded a little strange to me, but I agreed readily.

"Is there a place in a corner of the backyard where a large tree once stood?" he asked me.

"Yes, there were two trees removed by the previous owners."

"Bless these two spots as well," he instructed. "I don't know why, but there is something significant about one of these old trees."

I did all this the following night, and Lesa went out to a religious store and bought the crosses. Fr. Ron said that he would be getting back to me. This call seemed a little weird, because he was not inclined to answer any of my questions but only verified some information and gave me instructions. In retrospect it makes sense in light of the fact that he was working with Connie, and had to confer with her before he got back to me, but Fr. Ron had such an air of authority, even on the phone, that I would have stood on my head and prayed if he'd told me to. Fortunately for me he didn't.

Over the next week we all wore our crosses, but Bobby's cross didn't want to stay in place. Even though the chain was small enough that it couldn't fit over his head, it consistently came off while he slept. When he woke up in the morning the cross and chain would be on the floor. One morning it was nowhere to be found, and he and I finally discovered it between the mattress and box springs. Bobby became more and more uneasy, because each time we found the cross, the clasp was still closed. A few days later we found the cross both removed and folded in half upon itself, as if it had been placed in a vise and bent with pliers. With this last incident we belatedly decided to move Bobby out of the blue room. We moved

Bobby and his furniture into the fifth smaller bedroom on the second floor that had originally been a maid's linen and ironing room with a walk-in closet.

Fr. Mike was surprised about all of the interest and activity from the diocese.

"I wonder what they know about this house and if they're telling us everything?" he said with a hint of frustration and displeasure in his voice. "Why didn't Fr. Lengwin come and bless the house with salt himself?"

"I have no idea why. I'm just happy that he's involved. I see it as a very positive development."

At this point he asked me if there was any way I could find out some history on the house and its previous owners on my own. Being a former Intelligence officer, I know how to research, so I went to work searching old county records, speaking with the head of the Brentwood Historical Society and, most importantly, with an older woman whose family moved into the house in 1941. I discovered that the house was built during the years of 1909 and 1910 by a very well-known commercial builder in Pittsburgh. I went to the phone book and was surprised to find the company listed. I called and spoke with Roy, the president of the company, and he said that his grandfather had in fact built residential houses around the turn of the century. He invited me to stop by his office to see a picture of his grandfather with his crew standing in front of a house under construction. To my surprise, when I saw the picture, it was my house! It was commissioned to be built by Preston and Louise Malick. They purchased the lot for $5,800 and then borrowed $10,000 from a John Wagner that was secured by the value of the lot. John Wagner was a retail dealer in materials, and the loan was most likely for the cost of the building materials. Wagner was a prominent citizen in the small upscale community of Mount Oliver at the time, serving as the community's mayor.

Preston Malick was born in Erie County, Pennsylvania, in 1866, and his family had settled there around 1800. He was the owner of a large hardware store on Pittsburgh's South Side near the J&L Steel Mill. He became a leading citizen in Brentwood and even held public office for a time prior to 1920. In the picture he was a big man in a classic stiff Victorian pose.

In 1915 he sold his store and became the district manager for a large nail manufacturer and then in 1921 went to work for the American Steel and Wire Company. Mr. Malick retired in the 1930s, and the Great Depression appears to have left him unable to pay off the original $10,000 mortgage, so he was forced to convey the title to the house back to the widow of John Wagner. The house sat empty until 1941 when her son took possession. In addition to the mortgage, the Malicks apparently struggled to pay their taxes during the Depression, and it caused great local controversy and outrage that they were forced to give up their home to the Wagners.

I then made an appointment to speak with the daughter of the Wagner who took possession of the house in 1941. She was a sophisticated older woman who was ten when her family moved into the house. I met with her and her husband one evening in their living room and told her that I wanted to ask her some questions about the house.

"Have you or your family ever experienced anything of a 'spiritual' nature in the house?" I asked her, hopeful that she would be more open than the McHenrys.

She stared at me for a moment, then looked at her husband, looked back at me, and then, after a long pause, a smile came to her face and she said, "Oh yes, many times."

She described that not long after her family moved in they had a housewarming party for a number of their friends and all were gathered in the large expanse of the first floor. Later in the evening all of a sudden everyone heard a terrible racket coming from the second floor, slamming doors, pounding on the walls, and furniture moving about. Her father and several other men rushed to the second floor expecting to confront an intruder, but to their surprise they found no one. The whole company of guests then proceeded to search the second and third floors, expecting to find someone hiding in a closet or under a bed—but no one was there. That was their welcome into the house, and it was the first occurrence of a regular pattern of events that would be experienced over many years. She didn't give me too many details but did say that they regularly heard pounding on either the walls or closed doors, and loud footsteps in the hall and on the steps.

"There was one particular bedroom on the second floor at the top of the steps that we would not use as a bedroom. It was a 'sitting room only'" she told me. "It had a small door knocker on the door that we didn't understand," she continued. "My mother kept a blue vase in this room that was her prized possession. She told us we had to learn to live with this activity. Also our dog seemed to be able to sense the presence of a 'spirit' and would go from room to room apparently looking for it."

I surmised that when her mother eventually sold the house to the McHenrys, they weren't told about these issues associated with the house. Maybe this was the reason why Mrs. McHenry seemed to despise the Wagners. At the mention of their name, she proclaimed emphatically that she would never allow any of them to ever enter the house! We didn't ask why at the time, but now I thought that I had found the answer.

I then called Mr. McHenry to inquire if he might share with me what they had experienced during the nine years they had lived there. After a pleasant greeting, I asked him if we might get together for coffee and discuss some "interesting events" that had been taking place in the house. With that question, his tone immediately changed to a nervous one, and he quickly said that he would get back to me, and he hung up. I never expected him to call me back, and he never did.

CHAPTER THIRTEEN

Fr. Mike said that we should have prayers at the house again soon, and we scheduled his visit for the second week of July.

By this point, physical signs of the demon attacking us at night while we slept became a regular occurrence. Not only did I wake up with scratches nearly every morning, but before we moved him out of the blue room, Bobby was attacked with really nasty puncture wounds on his stomach. We took him to a doctor who said that it looked as if a dog had bitten him. Lesa had what appeared to be small puncture wounds on her left breast one morning, and David would occasionally have the long scratch marks on his chest that I was now experiencing on a regular basis.

Bobby finally seemed to have stabilized, but Charlie was beginning to exhibit some of the same traits. The demon apparently had shifted its attention, and over the coming months we would watch Charlie slide into his own pattern of disturbing self-destructive behavior, including severe depression, paralyzing anxiety, cutting himself with a razor, and even contemplating suicide.

Charlie had nightmares that felt real, dreams of being paralyzed. As he described it, "I wake up and I'm walking to the bathroom, and all of a sudden I freeze a foot off the ground. I try to scream but my lips are moving with nothing coming through them. I'm trying to fight it, I can't breathe, or move, I'm paralyzed."

It was at this point that an extremely disturbing event occurred that signaled to me that the battle was now going to a whole new level, possibly as a result of Fr. Ron being added to the team. I had spent the weekend at a men's retreat I'd organized at the Passionist monastery for local politicians, hoping it would help them work together more productively. I was still involved in local politics to a certain extent and knew many of Pittsburgh's leading politicians. During the retreat I also wanted to conduct a small experiment with my rosary beads. I was still using the crystal set with the silver cross that came from Medjugorje. I took them to the monastery with me and fell asleep saying the rosary in bed as usual. I awoke the next morning to find them at my side, lying there undisturbed. The links were not connected, as they would have been at home. I was actually relieved that they weren't, but then why would they have been? I was in a monastery. However, that night after I got home, as I was in the bedroom unpacking my overnight bag, I took the rosary out and laid them on my pillow. I went into the bathroom to take a bath as I usually did each night, and when I later went to get the rosaries to pray, I noticed that the crucifix was disfigured. As I examined it more closely I could see that it appeared to have been chewed as if it had been a toothpick! I could actually see the imprints of teeth at the bottom of the silver cross where it was smashed flat and twisted. The beads had not been linked together, and it was on my pillow where I had left it. The door to the room was still closed, and no one had come in or out. The beads had been in my bag since I left the monastery earlier in the day, and there was no plausible explanation even though I would have been happy to think of one. No, the demon had done this to send me a message. The battle for the house was about to intensify. It was intent on staying in the house, and it was going to fight us relentlessly. This was a demonstration of its power and its utter disdain for the tactics and rituals we were using.

But I still had confidence, the same type of confidence that I'm sure David had as he walked out to confront Goliath—certain that God was with him. Through it all, I was never terrified or horrified—very alarmed at times, but to me it was something that had to be taken care of, to be dealt with matter-of-factly. I wasn't sure how, but ultimately I knew the evil would be vanquished. Two days later Fr. Ron called. He told me to listen carefully and to do exactly what he said.

"There is an old antique mirror in the hallway on the second floor with a doorway immediately to the right [this doorway leads into the main bathroom]. I am not speaking about any of the mirrors above the fireplaces. I want you to take a black piece of cloth and cover that old mirror."

"Why?" I asked, stunned, because his description was

accurate to a T. There was an old mirror just where he said it was.

"Just do it," he responded. "All I can say now is that a story is beginning to take shape and I'll tell you about it when it becomes clearer to me."

"A story? What kind of story?"

"I see much blood in the bathroom and terrible things that once occurred in the basement. Keep an ample supply of holy water on hand, and request angelic support and protection while commanding the spirit to leave in the name of Jesus."

I told him how my rosary crucifix had been disfigured, as if it had been chewed, and asked him what he thought that meant.

"It's very disturbing, but it's in keeping with a crucifix that was once pounded with a mallet years ago in the basement." I had no idea what he was talking about.

He then further astonished me. He said that I should go out onto the front porch of the house after we were finished talking. As I was standing on the porch, looking out at the street, I should look to my left and across the street, and a block down I would see a house with a green door or green trim. I realized he was talking about the haunted house of my youth—the one with the door that mysteriously opened.

"That house is connected to yours," he told me. "There was a man who once owned it who did evil things in your house. He was responsible for a tremendous amount of blood and more deaths than could be counted. I see him with white gloves, a hat, and a cane with a manservant who accompanied him. The hat, gloves, and cane were always placed in the closet under the steps when he would visit your house, and the three rooms that stood out most as being associated with the blood were the bathroom, the blue room, and the furnace room."

"I don't have to look down the street, Father." I was awestruck. "You're talking about the doctor's house. I've heard tales of him more than once. Everyone's heard of Dr. M. He's a local legend. It's always been rumored that he performed illegal abortions in the 1920s and '30s and that's why that house is haunted."

When I was a kid I just knew it was the "haunted house," but when I grew older and became a councilman, with an interest in Brentwood history, the story was told to me on two separate occasions. It was said that the doctor would supposedly burn the remains in the coal furnace of the house. There were also tales of piles of cash hidden in the house and that the walls were once ripped open by intruders looking for it during the early 1960s. I actually spoke to a guy whose family rented it then, and they came home to find the place totally broken-up. He also told me of seeing white gloves, a hat, and a cane floating across the living room. His family moved out and the house sat empty for the next thirty years.

"This all fits," Fr. Ron responded. "The bedroom at the top of the steps next to the bathroom was used as a 'clinic' of sorts. Many illegal abortions were performed in that bedroom."

"You're talking about the room we call the 'blue room,' Father. It was Bobby's bedroom until recently."

"I see the body of a woman in a white dress who died at the bottom of the staircase. She wasn't married but had been sent there by a friend, an older man, a politician. She was put in a car and taken to the hospital. I also see another woman, screaming in pain, and a knocked over pan filled with blood."

He conveyed these horrifying scenes in his usual unemotional tone of voice. With this information, a pattern started to emerge: The bedroom, the furnace room, and the chair that always faced the fire door were linked to the abortion doctor and the financial problems of the Malicks, the family who built my house.

"When I see the bathroom I see a bathtub where a lot of blood has been disposed of," Fr. Ron related. "I see bloody sheets, bloody instruments, and bloody hands. These acts went on in this room for a number of years."

Fr. Ron would later tell me that he saw an initial abortion being performed for someone who lived in the house, either on one of the Malick women or possibly a servant girl. Possibly it was at this time that the convenient size and layout of the house was recognized by the doctor, which made it suitable for his secret abortion practice. The Malicks certainly needed the money he would pay them. It makes sense that he needed a secluded place away from his office or his own house where he could practice without fear of discovery. Because our driveway wrapped around to the back of the house, the women and vehicles could come and go unnoticed.

I later hired a historical specialist to do some research on Dr. M (as with the Malicks) and discovered that he was primarily a pediatrician who started to practice around 1915. He eventually operated what was referred to as a hospital, which served an area called the South Side Slopes, where mill workers and their families lived. This is actually on the side of a mountain that overlooked the J&L Steel Mill (now gone). I had a conversation with an older local businessman whose family has been in the funeral business for three generations, and he told me that he in fact knew Dr. M in his younger years. When he was a teenager (the doctor died in the late 1950s) his father would send him to the doctor's house to have death certificates signed. I asked him to describe Dr. M to me without any prompting, and this is what he said: "He was a very rough and profane old man who liked to drink, and always smelled of it. I never saw his wife but sometimes heard her in the background sounding drunk as well. He walked with a limp, and always wore a black hat, white gloves, and carried a cane. I didn't particularly like to be around the old guy and left as soon as I could." At this point Fr. Ron then presented me with a hard fact that I really didn't want to hear.

"Bob, this isn't going to be a short battle. There are no quick fixes against this level of evil. It will be months, possibly a year before we know if progress is being made against this demon. You need to make a decision, either move out of the house now or decide to stay and fight. It's going to be extremely difficult and your family may not be able to endure it." Fr. Ron's voice sounded strained. He knew he was giving me unwelcome news.

At this point I felt as if I were talking to Morpheus in the movie *The Matrix* and he was offering me the choice of taking the "red pill" or the "blue pill." The first option would rid us of the problem and hand it off to another unsuspecting family as it had been handed to us; the second option involved going down the rabbit hole so to speak. I had no idea what awaited us, but it sounded much worse than what we had already experienced. I did in fact now feel like I was living in the *The Matrix* where people don't have any idea that the world they inhabit is an illusion, that they are part of something much larger, darker, where they are being used as pawns of good and evil battling for control of them and their souls. I was now the one who was chosen to confront it in this particular place and time. I had to make the decision, and I made it then and there without a second thought. We were in. I didn't really know at the time what we were in for, and what lasting scars my family would suffer because of my choice.

I've been questioned and even criticized as to why I put my family through this horror. I did feel that I was protecting them, but they were in the middle of it, just as they had been during my battles in Brentwood. I couldn't sell the house to another family, and I was convinced that this evil could be overcome. But to be honest, this thing had challenged me for not only the possession of my house but my family, and my faith was such that I was prepared to die fighting. I was the focus of its hatred, and it knew that if it could break me, it could break the family and prevail, and it was correct in this assumption.

It wasn't all bad news. Fr. Ron also spoke of a "protective spirit" that was in the house with us as well but didn't elaborate.

"Will you come to the house now and help us?" I

asked him, feeling that his presence and his prayers would have great impact on the demon.

"I may, at some point, but the time isn't right yet." He later told me his presence would make the situation in the house worse. I didn't understand this but was encouraged that we seemed to be making some positive progress, or at least, we now better understood what was going on.

"Don't be disheartened, Bob. I'm going to consult with an exorcist in the Diocese of New York, and I'll get back to you with more information."

During this time the strange events began to escalate. One night as I was closing the window in our bedroom I found a round piece of metal not quite the size of a marble. It looked like an old musket ball and was covered in what appeared to be blood. It was in the windowsill where the window closes, and it made no sense how it got there. I asked everyone in the family if they had ever seen it, and no one had. It looked as if it would have been fired from a gun of the 1700s. Looking back, possibly it had something to do with the massacre I eventually would learn of.

Two days later Fr. Ron called again and asked me some more intriguing questions.

"Is there a large climbing rosebush in the right-hand corner of the backyard that grows on a trellis?"

"Yes, there is a rosebush there, but it grows over a white picket fence, not a trellis. In fact it grows precisely where one of the old trees we had spoken of earlier had once stood." This had to be more than coincidence.

"I'm pretty certain that the ashes of the remains were buried at the base of this tree," he said. "You should fashion a small cross out of wood and bury it at the base of this rosebush. And never bring roses from this bush into the house," he added in an emphatic tone of voice.

"This is interesting, Father. This bush produced beautiful pink roses for a number of years, but the rose color has turned to a deep blood red over the last year."

I buried the cross as he instructed and said a prayer for any deceased souls who might have been buried there as well. This all seemed a little bizarre to me at the time but would make perfect sense during the coming months. I couldn't get over the fact that he had "seen" the rosebush as well as the tree that had been cut down the year before we moved into the house.

The next day I related to Fr. Mike what Fr. Ron had told me.

"I'm sure he's not working from any information he has on the house," I told him.

"Well he's either consulting with a Christian mystic or he himself is one," Fr. Mike replied, long before Connie Valenti was revealed as the Christian mystic providing the information.

I could tell that Fr. Mike was taken aback by what I was telling him, but he was as intrigued as I was. This was going into a dimension that neither of us expected. We would have to come to grips with the power of pure evil. The battle would have to be fought in the supernatural realm and the physical concurrently. I prepared myself for the intense confrontation that I knew would soon be upon us. I didn't know it yet, but the house would become a battlefield in which individual rooms would be abandoned and eventually won back from the demon. We were preparing for war, and this evil thing was apparently doing so as well. Since we occupied the same space, it knew what I was doing, and I had to keep that in mind continuously.

Each escalation was brought on by new tactics by us or the demon. It would continuously come up with a new phenomenon to try to terrify us and convince us to pack up and leave. But once we became accustomed to the fact that it existed and was with us in the house, its mere existence no longer had that initial impact. We were just always wary as to what it would do next and how we would deal with it. It was like living with the Invisible Man. But most of all we wondered when it would end, and if, in fact, it ever would end.

I would have to figure this thing out by understanding its strengths and weaknesses, while at the same time learning how to effectively combat it on a supernatural level. Its primary weapon against us was overt terror tactics coupled with psychological oppression. I determined that we had to become numb to its terror and overcome its oppression with love for one another. That would be our defense. Our offense was yet to be determined but would come with time.

CHAPTER FOURTEEN

On my forty-eighth birthday, July 24, 2004, Fr. Ron called me to relate some very detailed instructions. I had great hopes that he had a winning plan, and initially, it seemed that way. But the dragon was clearly also ready to fight for its lair.

Fr. Ron felt that he had enough information about the situation in the house to direct a major counterblow. He told me that there was a "portal" of sorts in the house that had been opened years before by the many evil deeds that took place there. Or that the portal might be related to the land on which the house was built. As long as it was open, the demon or demons would continue to pass through it. He then went on to describe the process of a somewhat simple cleansing ceremony that I was to put together.

"Bob, you are to gather four priests and conduct this ceremony during the day when the house is empty."

His instructions were very precise. "You are to enter

the house holding a crucifix and a container of holy water. Once inside in a loud and forceful voice that can be heard throughout the house command: *This is my house. This is a holy house. This is a house of peace. This is a house of tranquility. All evil forces are to leave.*"

While I was doing this the four priests were to be standing outside at the four corners of the house praying. I was to then leave the house for a few minutes and say an "Our Father." At this point we were all to reenter the house and stand in the foyer in a circle facing out with our backs to one another. Each of us was to be holding a crucifix, a blessed candle, or holy water. At that point I was to repeat what I had said earlier, and each of the priests was to pray out loud as the spirit of God moved them.

"Then what?" I asked.

"You will know when it is time to conclude the ceremony," Fr. Ron said.

He also told me to remove the black cloth that had covered the mirror in the upstairs hallway for over a month.

"This ceremony will silence the evil spirit for a time, and we can determine the next steps later." That was all Fr. Ron had to say on the matter.

I was absolutely convinced that something important would occur as there was an air of great drama about this ceremony.

"Will Fr. Ron be attending this event?" Fr. Mike asked me the next day when I relayed to him all of the instructions.

"No," I told him, feeling somewhat uneasy about the cloak of mystery that remained around Fr. Ron. But there was nothing I could do about that.

"He told me his presence wouldn't be beneficial."

Fr. Mike was a little perturbed by this response but then took it in stride and we began to plan the event. Initially we discussed finding two additional Catholic priests to participate in this ceremony, and he suggested that I approach the local pastor of the Catholic church that was just a few blocks from the house. But the more I thought about it, the more I thought that wouldn't work. First of all, we were well into this situation, and finding new priests who would understand and be willing to get involved seemed too difficult at this point. I also did not want to take the chance that this situation could become public knowledge in the community.

The alternative was to use ministers that I already knew well and trusted. Two came to mind immediately. The first was John Guest, a legendary local pastor who was an internationally known evangelist as well. He is an ordained Episcopal priest who had established what has become known as a mega-church in metropolitan Pittsburgh. The second was also a well-known minister, pastor, and revered preacher of the First Presbyterian Church of Pittsburgh, the Reverend Leslie Holmes. Each had asked me to speak at their churches on different occasions.

John Guest is an impressive man who stands at least six feet three inches tall with an English accent that had not diminished despite several decades in the United States. He came to America during the sixties as part of a rock and roll band and still has that Paul McCartney look about him. Leslie Holmes is a shorter, stocky Scotsman whose deep Scottish brogue made his hard-hitting sermons even more powerful. I was confident that I could approach both with my situation and they would agree to help. I was right. Unfortunately, Leslie had just accepted a position in another city and was in the process of moving. He would not be available but told me that his assistant, another sturdy Scotsman, the Reverend David Brown, would be willing to take his place. David was a much younger man but had the spiritual weight and maturity required. He signed on immediately.

I approached another very well-known local Christian leader who, when he understood the serious nature of the situation, sounded very frightened and said he wanted nothing to do with it. I accepted his response but was surprised by this immediate and strong reaction. Maybe he'd had a prior experience with the demonic and was scared off.

However, I did now have four ministers including Fr. Ed. I asked Fr. Ron if it was OK to have Protestant ministers and well as Catholic priests.

"As long as the group is made up of men dedicated to God, that's all that counts," he told me. "Prayer and faith are just as strong whether they originate from a Protestant minister or a Catholic priest."

The date for the ceremony was set for Sunday, August 15, at 2:00 P.M. My friend Kerry also wanted to be involved, and again Fr. Ron said that it would be no problem as long as he recognized the gravity and potential danger associated with the event. We had no idea how the demon was going to react to the pressure brought to bear.

In the days leading up to the ceremony the evil entity became very active. My crystal rosary beads from Medjugorje, the ones on which the crucifix had been mutilated, were linked together to the point that it seemed fruitless to attempt to separate the links again.

Fr. Ron gave me some specific instructions to follow regarding these beads.

"Take the beads and immerse them in a new, small white glass bowl filled with holy water. Leave them in the water for fifteen to twenty minutes, take them out, and let them dry without wiping them with a cloth. Then break the bowl and immediately put it in the rubbish outside of the house."

"Why are these particular beads being targeted by the demon?" I asked.

"Demons hate rosary beads that are deemed to be 'holy.' They project a strong energy, which is received as 'pulsations of pain' as each bead in the loop is used to focus the mind and heart in prayer."

"Why connect them like that?"

"So they can't be used. These particular beads will have to be removed from the house at some point if the spirit continues to attack them," Fr. Ron told me.

"I'm prepared to do whatever is necessary, Fr. Ron. You know that."

The beads continued to be a target, and Fr. Ron later told me to take them and bury them at my mother's grave as a request for special intercessory prayers from her in Heaven. I can't say that I understood all that he was telling me, but I never questioned his wisdom. I simply followed instructions.

Then two days before the ceremony an even more disturbing event occurred, and unfortunately, it would

Gene and Flo. My parents during World War II in Washington, D.C.

Family photo circa 1995. Jessica, Bobby, David, and Charlie with proud parents Bob and Lesa Cranmer. *Used with permission.* ©*Lifetouch, Inc.*

Picture of the house in December 1988 with Bobby in front after the moving van left the day we moved in.

Unless otherwise noted, all photos are from the Cranmer Collection.

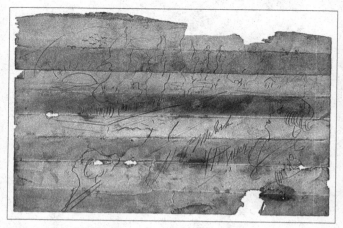

Happy scene of two women looking at a beautiful sunset in the backyard. Signed by Herbert Preston Malick.

Distorted drawing of Mr. Malick with a large extended nose, including a man laughing at him, a pig's head, and a coiled snake lunging to strike Malick. It also includes what appears to be an altar or font.

The light with a pull chain is clearly seen with a rosary still attached. Opening in the wall is a section that was cut out.

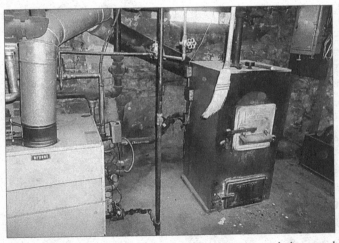

Gas boiler with a supplemental wood boiler. An extremely large coal boiler once sat here fed by a supply screw from the coal room.

Above: View looking down from the third-floor landing through the second floor to the first-floor staircase.

Right: Collin during the struggle.

Picture I took of Sandy's "terminal stare" as I was unknowingly standing up close and personal with the entity.

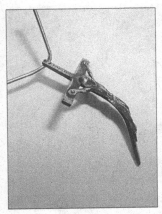

Left: This crucifix I never took off, becoming bent as I wore it.

Right: The St. Benedict Crucifix is one of the oldest and most honored medals used by Catholics due to the belief in its power against evil. It is also known as the "devil-chasing medal." I kept it at my bedside.

The first blood that appeared. Unfortunately, the camera flash masked the dramatic images to a degree.

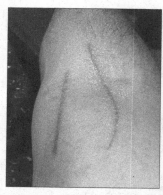

Right: Some very routine scratches on my arm. Usually they appeared in a group of three. These two appeared to be made one at a time.

Middle: The living room today. This is where Mass was repeatedly celebrated and prayers said.

Bottom: Space where final scene with the entity was played out—far right corner of the room.

Scan of the grave site being conducted. Jacob Lammott, project manager from Ground Penetrating Radar Systems Inc.

Actual boundaries of the grave marked by the ground penetrating radar survey.

Area in the yard where the remains of a four-person grave was discovered. A sapling oak tree was planted there as a memorial.

Lesa and I never moved back to the master bedroom, preferring the new peaceful feel of the formerly ominous blue room.

A picture of the house taken in 2013 from Sceneridge Avenue, an adjacent street off Brownsville Road.

become a daily occurrence in the months to come. We were struck with the terrible stench of sulfur and burning rubber in the master bedroom on the second floor, a room that we had transformed into a second-floor living room. It was much stronger than usual. You could almost reach out and touch it, it was so concentrated in certain spots. The smell was so powerful that it remained in your nostrils for some time after you left the room. Plus it moved around. Eventually I went into the room and said in a loud voice, "In the name of Jesus I command you to leave this room." With that the smell immediately went away completely. Charlie was with me and witnessed the event. Unfortunately, forcing the smells to depart would become much more difficult.

When I reported the smells to Fr. Ron, he reassured me, "This is not all bad news, Bob. It's an indication that the spirit is aware you are planning to strike back and is experiencing anxiety and dread."

That made me feel somewhat relieved. It meant we weren't helpless, that we could strike back at this thing and win—that it was vulnerable. It may have been doing its best to terrorize us at the moment, but I had faith that if we stood firm and marshaled the forces of righteousness, we'd give it more than it could handle.

The problem was persevering until we could make that happen.

Bumping and pounding in the house continued unabated during the days prior to the ceremony, but instead of being demoralized I continued to take it as a sign of the coming battle—that the spirit was attempting to scare us off. I asked Fr. Mike to bring a number of blessed candles with him to the house so I could use them in certain rooms of the house if the battle persisted, but I hoped that it would end as a result of the concentrated prayer ceremony.

When the appointed day arrived, I was filled with much anticipation and courage. I didn't know what to expect, but I was anxious to get to work. I felt that this one great thrust just might be enough to push this evil thing out the door forever.

It was a beautiful, sunny Sunday afternoon. Lesa had gone shopping and the kids were with friends. Fr. Ed pointed out to me that the day I had selected was the Feast of the Assumption of the Blessed Mother of Jesus. To me this coincidence made things all the better. Everyone arrived on time, and it was an impressive sight: two Catholic priests, an Episcopal priest, and a Presbyterian minister, all decked out in their formal religious garb. We gathered on the front porch of the house for a half hour or so and reviewed the instructions we had received from Fr. Ron. The two ministers and Fr. Ed had crucifixes, Fr. Mike had the holy water, and Kerry and I each had a blessed candle.

As I entered the house alone I drew great courage from the men of God who surrounded the house giving prayers of support. I heard sounds of movement on the second floor as I made my pronouncements, and I could feel that the thing was upset and chose to hide rather than fight as it had done in the past. I was sure it was confused as to why its terror tactics weren't working. As

I left the house I fully expected to hear some type of loud crash, but there was nothing. All of us reentered the house and formed the appointed circle in the foyer, and each of the ministers began to pray out loud one after the other. The tension was very high, and I expected at any time that something would happen, but nothing did. The ceremony continued for about twenty-five minutes and then it was over. There were no sounds or rumblings, and afterward we all gathered again on the front porch to talk. That was it; no thunder, no crashes, just a calm peace. We all went to the second floor and I removed the black cloth that had covered the mirror. We also discussed what manifestations had recently occurred in the house. I eventually thanked everyone for their participation and they all left.

He didn't mention it to me at the time, but I later received an email from the Presbyterian minister, David Brown, telling me that as he had stood outside Bobby's recently vacated bedroom (the blue room) he was aware of an "oppressive" force emanating from it at least two feet from the doorway. He said that it was a "heavy and soporific" feeling.

Lesa returned a short time later, and we settled in to see what would happen, or if anything would. I had a feeling at the time that the thing was merely hiding upstairs somewhere and that it would eventually reemerge to make its presence known. Unfortunately my feelings were correct. The elaborate ceremony ended up being more like D-day, in which we established a beachhead but still had a long slog of messy battles ahead of us. Just like the Nazis in

Normandy, this evil force was not going to give up ground easily, and in fact would launch many counterblows of its own to push us out.

Fr. Ron called me later that evening and we had a long discussion.

"The ceremony you held this afternoon with the holy men was very powerful, Bob. The demon spirit has never experienced anything like it before. You've given it notice that it's involved in a serious battle and that its usual tactics of terror will not be sufficient to drive you out."

"I hope you're right, Father. I was expecting some kind of sign of victory, something to happen. But nothing did. It was somewhat disappointing."

"Does the room on the second floor where the terrible stench occurred have wallpaper with vertical blue stripes and a green flowered design on it?" he asked, changing the subject.

"It has exactly that design," I answered, impressed again by the accurate description.

"There's something in the room that's giving off a powerful level of negative energy. You need to find it," he said.

I told him that I would look and went to the room. I looked around at the furniture and opened the drawers of an end table and Lesa's dresser and found nothing out of the ordinary. I then moved to my chest of drawers. In one of the drawers I found what I felt was the source of the negative energy Fr. Ron was referring to. When I was a teenager my mother was an amateur antique dealer, and

I would go with her to many different antique flea markets. I had developed a hobby of collecting WWI and WWII medals and artifacts and had purchased a number of German medals, Nazi armbands, and flags. A few years later I came to fully understand what it all represented and ended up giving the items away to another collector. However, I did keep one medal that was associated with the German panzer divisions. This medal is made up of a tank with a wreath around it and, like most items from that era, has the dreaded swastika on it.

I called Fr. Ron and told him what I had found.

"This is what you need to do with it, Bob. Simply seal it in a small box and affix a wooden cross on top of it." I did that as soon as we got off the phone.

"Is there a beautiful red and blue vase on a dark table in the hallway next to Bobby's bedroom? It's very special to someone."

Again, I was astonished by his description. In fact there was an antique vase that had belonged to my mother on a small wooden table in the hallway between the bathroom door and Bobby's bedroom.

"This is an object with very positive energy," he told me. "You should fill it with roses." There happened to be a half dozen roses growing on a bush located in the front yard (far from the burial site bush in the backyard), so I did that as well.

I was filled with foreboding when Fr. Ron ended our conversation by saying, "Expect activity from the demon at the end of the coming week as it recovers and regains its strength."

CHAPTER FIFTEEN

Things were quiet during the week after the deliverance ceremony just as Fr. Ron had said they would be. But like clockwork the following Saturday night, activity started again with a bang—or rather a pop. Lesa and I came home about 11:30 P.M., and as I stood in the foyer there was an extremely loud pop just as if someone had broken a large lightbulb next to me. Lesa came running out from the kitchen in the rear of the house, thinking that I had knocked something over. She found me standing there looking around for broken glass, fallen plaster, but nothing was amiss. The demon was toying with me again.

I was never sure what each day would bring regarding the demon's activity. It had the run of the house and would move pictures and furniture and constantly attempt to unnerve our minds. As already described, clocks would stop, the computer would freeze, appliances would malfunction, and my watch even stopped running. During 2004 and 2005 the blue room was the focal point of my attention. This room was a key to the battle, and I knew that if the house was to be healed, the blue room would have to be cleansed.

Fr. Ron said that we should expect the spirit to come back at us strongly at some point, so I decided that we might as well plan to strike first. Fr. Ron called and told me of a revelation in which a "bloody bathtub" was seen and money was being passed from the doctor to the original owners of the house. His last revelation was the most unsettling. He said we should expect at some point to actually see blood running down the walls caused by the demon. He would always end his communications with "May you have a gentle and joy-filled day!" and I would think to myself, "Yeah, right!"

It was about this same time that Fr. Mike began to speak with another Catholic mystic by the name of Barb. She would periodically provide her insight as to what was going on in the house, and even though it wasn't as detailed as what Fr. Ron described, it generally supported his revelations. She indicated there were "old sins" in the house and that the evil associated with those sins was still present. She specifically pointed to the sins of adultery, hatred, and violence, rape, séances, spirit channeling, and deceit. She said that she was overwhelmed by the amount of wickedness occupying the house. Barb would add revelations occasionally during the coming months, and she did visit once. I've been told since that she has the gift of the stigmata suffering in her palms and feet, and that it had been verified by the Church.

In September 2004 after the ceremony I would begin

to say the rosary each night aloud in the blue room with blessed candles burning, occasionally burning blessed incense as well. I also came upon another plan of attack for continuous cleansing. Lesa and I set up a television in the room with a DVD player attached. We purchased a copy of Mel Gibson's movie *The Passion of the Christ* and put it on repeat mode. The movie played twenty-four hours a day for the next seven months. At least once or twice a week we would find that either the television or the DVD player had been turned off during the day and sometimes the DVD would actually be removed, but we would simply turn it on once again and let it play. Later on when we had to abandon the master bedroom on the second floor we had the movie playing simultaneously during the day in both rooms. I also had cassette tapes of Bishop Wuerl praying the rosary, which I would play at times, but I was unable to have it repeat automatically like *The Passion* movie. I must say that I have watched that movie so many times that I know each and every scene and word of dialogue. I considered it a particularly effective weapon because it so graphically displayed the crucifixion and the blood Christ shed for our sins. (Despite Mr. Gibson's personal issues after its completion, his movie is considered by many to be a powerful and Biblically accurate representation.) The greatest weapon against the Devil is the blood of Jesus, per the New Testament. And since the blood of innocents had been shed in the house, I felt that a movie about the blood of Christ was very appropriate. When Lesa would be harassed by the spirit during the day when she was home alone, she would simply tell the thing to go and watch the movie!

There was no question that we could no longer use the blue room. It was the evil heart of the house, which is probably why Bobby had been so negatively affected when he slept and spent time in it. But since we'd all moved out of the blue room, at this point the demon manifested itself mostly in a room across the hall that it perceived as belonging to me and planned to possess.

I had transformed what was the master bedroom into a second-floor living room of sorts, with a fireplace, art on the walls, and a television. I had also reinstalled a door and a sunporch, which had originally sat on the back flat roof. I would go there in the evenings, generally around 7:30 to 8:00 P.M. each night. The demon began to occupy the room at about 7:00 P.M. with its hideous stench so I would be unable to use it. It would always be waiting for me after dinner. A nightly battle would ensue as I would attempt to expel it from the room with a whole series of prayers and commands for it to leave. At first Lesa would assist me, and we would pray the rosary out loud together, interactively saying the "Hail Mary." But after a while this became too much for her and I would pray out loud by myself, following the thing around the room armed with a crucifix and hitting it with holy water from a container. As time went on the process would become more and more onerous, and on a number of occasions, if after several hours it didn't leave, I would simply give up and go downstairs. It became a nightly test of endurance between us. Some nights I won; some nights it won. This went on for several months as a regular routine.

As I've mentioned before, I was not the only one the presence liked to torment. One day when Charlie was home after school alone in his room, his door was locked from the outside. The old wooden doors have manual turn-bolt locks on the inside and can only be locked from the outside with a key. Since they all took old skeleton-type keys, we only had keys for one or two of the doors, and his bedroom wasn't one of them. He eventually got out through a window that leads onto the roof sunporch.

Our family hunkered down during this period, and we simply learned to endure what was going on around us. Most of the activity was now centered on the second floor, where two rooms were basically empty and the movie was playing constantly with the doors closed to each. Lesa and I had a bedroom, Charlie and David were in theirs, and Bobby was in the small "maid's room." Charlie and Bobby both were still afflicted with anxiety, but each was seeing a therapist and on medication. They were getting better slowly. Bobby had calmed down and was no longer violent. David was fine and even seemed to grow bolder as he could sense what I was going through. He wanted to help me, but I usually told him that I had it covered and appreciated his concern.

With all that was now occurring in the house I was becoming increasingly uneasy about Jessica and Collin. The activity at this point had stopped on the third floor, but I knew that it could flare up again at any point. The rational side of me wanted to move them out, while the warrior in me said no. I would not yield or retreat; it would leave, not us. This was my house, my family. My uncompromising attitude prevailed but would soon be forced to adjust. In warfare retreat by design is often necessary.

I would speak with Fr. Ron on the telephone almost

every night as well. Many times he would call as I was up in the room doing battle and I would call him back exhausted when it was over, often well after 11:00 P.M. He didn't care what time of the day or night I called. He was always there to give me support and encouragement. There is no question in my mind that without him being in my corner between rounds to give me direction and attention, I never could have continued with the fight. I felt like he was telling me, *"Okay, kid, you're doing good. Cover up and keep moving!"*

The daily rigor of this confrontation is hard for me to comprehend now, years later, but it did occur exactly as I describe it. The demon fought relentlessly, but so did I. I no longer assumed that just because my opponent was a being with supernatural powers it was stronger than I was, for I had supernatural powers at my disposal as well. The power of the Lord and his holy angels was with me, as were the prayers of the Passionist nuns and all of the weapons and learning of the Catholic Church. I was confident that I had an arsenal at my disposal; I just had to have the will to stand firm and use it.

I knew that if the demon spirit was fighting back that it was also being weakened, and if it could be weakened it could be beaten, and if it could be beaten I would continue to fight, and continue fighting until we won.

CHAPTER SIXTEEN

I asked Fr. Mike and Fr. Ed if we could plan an evening when we would celebrate Mass and say the rosary at the house. The date selected for the Mass was September 8, 2004, which again, by coincidence, was the feast day of the birth of Mary the mother of Jesus. I thought that this was significant since we would be celebrating Mass in the blue room. Everyone arrived at the house promptly at 6:00 P.M. Lesa and I and the three boys were joined by Fr. Ed, Fr. Mike, and Kerry.

I had the altar set up in the room along with a circle of chairs. Both of the priests said the Mass, while Lesa and I participated by doing the assigned readings. We all partook of Holy Communion, and it turned into a very peaceful and fulfilling holy celebration. Following the Mass we all went downstairs and ate a dinner that Lesa had prepared while we talked. After dinner the two priests, Kerry, and I went back to the blue room to participate in the praying of the rosary led by Fr. Ed. This, as well, was an undisturbed, solemn event.

When we were done Kerry sniffed the air and said, "Do you smell that?"

"What are you talking about?" I asked him. I thought I'd caught a faint whiff of a floral odor but wasn't sure.

"There's an overpowering smell of roses in the room, Bob. It's strange that you can't smell it. It smells like a flower shop in here." Fr. Ed then told us that the presence of the Blessed Mother often coincides with the smell of flowers.

We were feeling rather lifted up by the whole experience of Mass, the rosary, and the pleasant scent until we walked out into the hallway and into my second-floor living room where we were struck with the overpowering rancid stench of sulfuric burning rubber. Everyone could smell it as it moved around the room. We all formed a circle at the center of the room and prayed aloud and it disappeared. The priests and Kerry left the house a half hour later, and I went upstairs again to discover that the rancid smell had returned even stronger than it had been before. I took the candles off the altar we had used for Mass and carried them into the room with me along with a bottle of holy water. I located where the stench was the strongest and began to sprinkle that space with the holy water, commanding the thing to leave the room in the name of Jesus. This went on for a while until the smell went away completely. I anointed the door to the room with holy oil and went downstairs to recover from this confrontation. The smell was so strong that it made me nauseous.

Lesa had been downstairs during this, and I described to her what had occurred. That night before I went to bed I set up the television and the DVD player in the room where the stench had been to play *The Passion of the Christ* movie throughout the night. The next morning when I left the house at about 6:00 A.M. it was still playing. When Lesa got up about an hour later and walked down the hall to wake up Charlie, she discovered large drops of foamy liquid on the hardwood floor leading away from the entrance of his room to the room where the stench had been and the movie was playing. She cleaned it up and told me about it later in the morning. I called Fr. Ron and he simply said that the demon was extremely angry at what had taken place the night before.

Things began to get worse with the boys again. The same day Lesa was cleaning up the foamy liquid, which she later identified as smelling like birth fluid, she found a notebook belonging to Charlie hidden under his mattress. She had been going through his room for clues to his mental state. In it was a completed suicide note. Fr. Ron advised me to check with his doctors as to the medicine he was on, as it may have been too strong. After Lesa found the note, the crucifix and chain she was wearing around her neck simply fell to the floor without being uncoupled. She later talked to his therapist about the note, and his medication was in fact changed.

The next day Fr. Ron called me with a load of information that was hard for me to comprehend all at once.

He told me that he (actually Connie, I would discover

years later) had visualized what he called a "door of sorrows" in the back of the house through which the women who were seeking the illegal abortions entered and left. A few years earlier we'd decided to remove the inner walls of the closed-in porch off the dining room to add insulation (this was the kids' TV room). In doing so, we discovered a glass-paneled door completely encased inside the wall facing the back of the house. It had simply been covered up at some point. Apparently there had been a set of wooden steps at the time to access the door, and it still looked to be in working order. Instead of removing it I decided to insulate over it and simply built out a little to accommodate the thick insulation and a new wall.

I had thought nothing of it until Fr. Ron brought it up. He said that one of the attractions of the house was that the driveway wrapped around the back of the house and the women could come and go discreetly because of this rear entrance. This was in fact the "door of sorrows" that had been seen in the vision. Fr. Ron went on to describe that this doctor was very rough and rude with the women and treated them terribly. He was often drunk when he did his work and made many mistakes, taking no care at all for sanitary conditions. The demon feasted on all of this pain and anguish.

"This is the reason Bobby was specifically affected by the spirit," he continued. "There were some issues he had when he was born."

"Well, he experienced a very difficult birth, Father. He was what the doctor called a blue baby. He swallowed a lot of fluid and his breathing stopped. They worked on him quite a while before he could breathe on his own. I was very alarmed when they ran out of the delivery room with him. So what does it mean?" I asked.

"Bobby came very close to death and thus he has a sensitive spirit similar to the many that died in the house," Fr. Ron explained. "He barely escaped death; the many others in that house weren't as fortunate as he."

"Then why was Lesa a target?" I asked.

"Simply because she's a woman who has given birth to four children. If there is a portal to evil in a specific place it will feed on the death of innocents and bring pain and anguish to mothers in the process. Many children died in and around that house."

We had *The Passion* playing in both rooms at this point nonstop, and the rancid smell appeared and disappeared on the second floor during the day as well while Lesa was home alone. The chain in the coat closet began to wrap around the light again even though I stood in the doorway and commanded it to stop and then blessed the closet with salt and anointed the door with oil.

Jessica, who was at this time four months pregnant with her second child, began to experience sharp pains in her stomach. Lesa took her to the hospital, but apparently everything was alright once she left the house. Even though the spiritual activity was no longer on the third floor where she, her husband, and Collin were living and seemed to be confined to primarily the second floor, the spirit seemed to be confused and angry. I became very concerned. I thought it was being affected by the contin-uous playing of the movie in two rooms along with the commands and prayers it was constantly confronted with. I continued to extol the power of Jesus to expel and bind the demon along with references to the Blessed Mother of Jesus and the Archangel Michael to cleanse the house. I wasn't certain if we were winning or losing, but I felt empowered.

Fr. Ron advised me to take one of the blessed candles and walk through the entire house praying aloud, which I did. It seemed to respond to my commands when confronted, which was a positive development until the astonishing occurrence of September 18, 2004.

It was a Saturday morning and I had attended Mass at the Passionist convent as I usually did on Saturday. At around 9:30 A.M. I was in the kitchen with Lesa having coffee. As I walked through the dining room earlier I had noticed the faint smell of the demon, but by now the putrid stench was somewhat burned into my nostrils so I paid little attention to it. Our son David—who, miraculously, did not seem to be affected by the evil spirit at all, even when he woke up occasionally with scratches down the center of his chest—was in the TV room on the couch. From his vantage point he could see directly through the dining room into the entrance to the kitchen. He walked into the kitchen and asked us, "Where did that person go and who was it?"

"What person?"

"I just saw someone at the kitchen door wearing a black robe or a dress," he told me.

"What did they look like?" I asked.

"It had jet-black hair down to the shoulders so I couldn't see its face. It walked into the doorway of the kitchen and then turned and walked over toward where you and mom were sitting so I lost sight of it. I came in to see who it was."

He wasn't excited or upset, because it looked so real that he was sure someone was in the kitchen with us. I was taken aback at first but then understood what had happened.

"The thing is upset and is now doing all it can to intimidate us," I told him.

"Well, it doesn't frighten me," David said boldly.

"That's good," I told him. "This thing feeds on fear, and if it can't scare you, it loses a lot of its power. Laugh at it and you'll drive it crazy."

Fr. Ron called later and I told him about the incident.

"It's a very encouraging sign that it specifically singled out David, who isn't affected by its tactics," Father said. "He may be ready to help confront it as well."

The following night I went upstairs around 9:00 P.M. and, as usual, the demon spirit was already in my room waiting for me. I called Lesa up to assist me, and we decided to confront this thing as hard as we could. We closed the door to the room and each of us lit a blessed candle. The stench was strong and pervasive but confined to one part of the room so we could determine exactly where it was. We stood facing each other with the demon between us and I hit it with holy water.

"We are not frightened by you," I said loudly. "You cannot terrify us and you *will* be expelled through the power of the cross of Jesus."

We then sat down and proceeded to pray the rosary interactively with the stench still hanging heavy in the room. I darkened the lights so that the room was primarily lit by our two candles. We were not frightened and drew strength from the prayers we were repeating:

I believe in God, the Father Almighty, Creator of Heaven and earth and in Jesus Christ, His only Son, our Lord; Who was conceived by the Holy Spirit, born of the Virgin Mary, suffered under Pontius Pilate, was crucified, died, and was buried, He descended into Hell; the third day He arose again from the dead; He ascended into Heaven, sitteth at the right hand of God, the Father Almighty, from thence He shall come to judge the living and the dead. I believe in the Holy Spirit, the Holy Catholic Church, the communion of saints, the forgiveness of sins, the resurrection of the body, and life everlasting. Amen.

Our Father, Who art in Heaven, hallowed be Thy name; Thy Kingdom come, Thy will be done on earth as it is in Heaven. Give us this day our daily bread; and forgive us our trespasses as we forgive those who trespass against us; and lead us not into temptation, but deliver us from evil. Amen.

Glory be to the Father, the Son, and the Holy Spirit. As it was in the beginning is now and ever shall be, world without end. Amen.

O my Jesus, have mercy on us. Forgive us our sins. Save us from the fires of Hell. Take all souls into Heaven, especially those most in need of thy mercy. Amen.

Hail Mary, full of grace, the Lord is with thee, blessed art thou amongst women and blessed is the fruit of thy womb, Jesus. Holy Mary Mother of God, pray for us sinners now and at the hour of our death. Amen.

It then moved from this room through the open door into our bedroom, and we followed it there as well. Once there it moved back into the sitting/living room again, and Lesa sat down on the floor in the doorway between the rooms to try to corral it between us. I continued to sprinkle it with holy water when I could locate it, and eventually the stench died out after almost two hours of confrontation.

After that session we went downstairs and took a break, mentally and emotionally spent. Then it dawned on me that this thing was trying to take over our rooms while we should be concerned with cleansing the blue room. I now realized that all of this time its "heart" was actually in the blue room and it was moving around trying to divert and confuse us. So we went into that room and said the rosary as well. Finally, after a long and stressful night we went to bed well past midnight with no sign of the stench anywhere.

CHAPTER SEVENTEEN

The next day Fr. Mike decided that it was prudent, in light of all that was going on, to have another session in the house that week. It would be a full-fledged deliverance session once more with both priests and, as usual, Kerry, too. The next morning after I left for work Lesa told me that the stench was present throughout the second floor again. That evening thankfully there was no sign of it, but the next evening it was back in force with a suffocating fog that made my sitting room unusable. By that point, I wasn't using it anymore, and we had since moved all of the furniture out of the room.

It was clear the demon was now waging an escalating attack upon us. We didn't know what would happen next or how long this assault would last. Could its power to continue match our will to persevere, and would we be able to persevere long enough to expel it? Maybe I could face off against this evil thing, but what about my family?

Lesa was home with it during the day, and it had had its way with her psychologically in the past. Then there were the boys. It had a grip on Bobby and Charlie, and I never knew what to expect next from them. And there was Collin to worry about as well.

That evening when I came home from work Lesa and I were in the kitchen eating dinner and watching the news. The phone rang. It was Jessica calling from the third floor. She told us she was sending two-and-a-half-year-old Collin downstairs to visit with us and he would be down in a minute. I paid the call little attention as I was fixated on the television. About a minute later I heard what sounded like the loud gasps of a child who was drowning. The television was on, but I still heard the sounds all the way from the front of the house. I immediately ran to the steps and up to the second-floor balcony landing to find little Collin standing in front of the blue room shaking like a leaf and gasping for air.

"Monster, monster will get me," he panted, as he pointed to the blue room. His face was a mask of fright, eyes bulging out of their sockets in a frozen stare! His mouth was wide open as if he was trying to scream but couldn't. Because of his developmental issues he could not yet verbalize fully what had occurred. (Collin, now twelve, will still not venture to the second floor by himself. He's not sure why but vaguely recalls the "black monster" that lunged out of the room at him.)

Lesa carried him downstairs and I felt like an idiot. I knew exactly what had happened and I was angry at myself for being so stupid. Here we were in the middle of a battle with a supernatural being and I had let my grandson walk alone right through the middle of the battlefield! What was I thinking? How could I have been so reckless and shortsighted?

I went into the blue room and said in a loud, firm voice, "I've had enough of you. You are a coward, going after a child." In my mind I could almost hear it laughing at me. Why would it care if I called it a coward? It was all about hurting, terrorizing, and if possible, killing innocent children. I felt foolish and, at that moment, impotent against it. I realized that it had accomplished its purpose; it had scored a direct hit on me. When the stench wafted over me I knew it had just experienced a major victory. It had found my greatest weakness.

When I regained my composure, I went downstairs to where Lesa was holding Collin, who was still trembling. The demon was upstairs stinking up the place, and I knew that it would probably soon be back on the third floor as well. It remained on the second floor throughout the evening, but I didn't attempt to confront it. It had won that day, and I was not in the right state of mind to attempt to fight with it. I was clearly too unsettled and angry and wasn't sure what to do. I was deeply wounded as well.

This was Tuesday and we were scheduled to have the priests back for Mass Thursday night. I had to go out of town the next day and would be returning Thursday afternoon before the Mass. I hoped that with me out of the house, things might settle down a bit. Lesa told me she felt she could handle being alone. *The Passion* continued to play, and I was confident that the unrelenting pressure was pushing the demon to these desperate acts.

The short time out of the house would also give me a much-needed break. The next day my boss and president of the company could tell that I was preoccupied.

"Bob, what's bothering you? You look distracted."

"Things have gotten a lot worse with the house," I told him. "That thing came after my grandson last night." I realized that he was not only my boss but my friend. He was one of the few people in whom I had confided as far as what we were going through, and quite frankly I needed someone to talk to.

"You need to get Collin out of the house," he said, looking worried.

"You're right," I said, knowing it was true. "I agree that's the only solution since I can't protect him."

Once again, I talked to my friend Tom Murphy, who happened to own a duplex a short distance from our house, one side of which had just become available. I could easily afford the monthly rent, and he was happy to help me out yet again. Jessica said she was ready to go because she was worried about Collin as well. I wondered why I hadn't done this earlier. I suppose I'd fooled myself into believing that I had things under control. I didn't, and felt foolish. I realized I'd been caught by surprise because it seemed like we were making progress and things had been moving in our direction, that we were in fact "winning." I'd become overconfident and been completely outmaneuvered.

When I arrived home Thursday evening I went upstairs to unpack and found a school notebook balanced on the rail of the banister overlooking the foyer. It had been left there for me to find. On the cover was "Charlie Cranmer," and in the address portion was one word: HELL. Charlie told me that he had not left it there but that it had been in his room. He said that he had recently written HELL on it because he felt as though that's where he lived because of the spirit wreaking havoc on our lives.

When the two priests arrived at 7:00 P.M. we all sat on the front porch: Lesa, Kerry, myself, and my son David. Charlie and Bobby were gone, and quite frankly I didn't want them there anyhow. We reviewed in detail what had occurred since the last Mass in the blue room: the daily confrontations, the foam on the floor, David's sighting in the kitchen, as well as what had happened with Collin two nights before. Fr. Mike then lit the incense pot and we began to walk around the outside of the house as he prayed openly. He spent extra time over the rosebush in the backyard, and then we entered the rear of the house through the kitchen door. We started in the basement and then went through the first floor, stopping in front of the wall that enclosed the "door of sorrows."

We then went to the second floor and spent a considerable amount of time in the sitting/living room that the spirit had taken possession of. The two priests prayed, and the incense so filled the room that it seemed as though it was on fire. But through the heavy odor of the incense we all were able to smell the sweet aroma of roses in the room as well. I was overcome with what I felt was the presence of holy angels and felt compelled to fall to my knees and pray in the center of the room. We then proceeded to go throughout the remainder of the house, including the third floor, and finally reassembled on the front porch. Jessica brought Collin out, and Fr. Mike blessed him with holy water. David and Jessica then carried him back up to the third floor.

We were all feeling like we had just won a great victory because of the smell of roses, but, to our utter dismay, when David came back down to the porch, he said that he was sorry to tell us that the rancid smell was now extremely strong on the second floor in the same room. We all went back upstairs, and as he had said, the smell was so strong it overpowered the lingering scent of the incense. We were able to isolate the smell in one corner of the room, so we all joined arms and surrounded it. We prayed while Fr. Mike hit it with holy water, and I started the tape of Bishop Wuerl reciting the rosary playing in the background. We stayed in this position for almost a half hour until the rancid smell began to dissipate.

When they all left the house that night I called Fr. Ron and reported to him what had occurred.

"Go down to the basement, Bob, and bless the furnace area with holy water. But be careful not to be pushed from behind as you go down the steps."

"Why? What happened in the furnace?"

"Many of the children that were aborted were late-term," he explained. "Their bodies had to be burned completely and the bones mixed with coal cinders. These remains were then disposed of in the backyard where the rosebush is. The doctor's hired man did this ghastly work. The doctor would also do some of his cleaning up in the basement laundry tub sinks, the three large ones."

This was where Jessica and Lesa had complained of

smelling the strong stench of amniotic fluid when doing the laundry—and in fact there are three tubs as he once again rightly noted.

The next week a pregnant Jessica and her little family moved out of the house. There seemed to be a brief lull in the battle, which lasted for a few days, and I was satisfied that we had made some significant progress and taken the appropriate measures. I continued my daily prayers, and *The Passion* continued to play in two rooms. Fr. Ron reminded me that this brief respite would only be temporary and that there was a lengthy struggle ahead of us. I welcomed the break and began to prepare myself for what he said was coming. I knew that the night when we prayed and said the rosary in the blue room the battle had been engaged. We were now left to either fight it out to the end or retreat. I felt better that Jessica's new baby—still in the womb—and Collin were out of the house. I was considering moving the boys out as well. If I ended up in the house alone that was fine with me. I would continue the battle until victory and peace were achieved and this demon was expelled. I went to the convent and asked the nuns to continue to pray for me.

Lesa now complained of a birth fluid smell that she said followed her around the house. The mysterious puddles continued to appear in the foyer and in the hallway on the second floor on a daily basis. Soon these fluid puddles would turn into a bloodlike substance, sometimes red and other times a rusty orange color. I could not smell it but it made Lesa sick. She then began to experience a serious pain in her right arm and neck that seemed to come from nowhere.

"This pain is the same as I felt that time I fell down the stairs just after we moved in. Remember?" she asked me and Jessica as we sat at the kitchen table one night while Jessica was visiting. "My legs were swept out from under me as I was coming down the steps, as if someone had pushed me. I slid down the steps to the landing and twisted my arm and hurt my back and neck." Lesa rubbed her arm where it hurt. "I looked up to see who had pushed me, but of course there was no one there."

"Don't you remember, Mom, that I fell exactly the same way once when I was pregnant with Collin?" Jessica reminded her. Lesa nodded. "I fell down the steps out of nowhere; my feet got swept out from under me. Thankfully I landed on my rear and not my back like you."

During that week Lesa called me at work and said the smell of the amniotic fluid was now so strong in the main bathroom that she couldn't go in without wanting to throw up. Our dog, Sandy, also began to sleep on the floor at night directly in front of our bedroom door and not next to our bed on his pillow like he usually did. He would now wake me up at night on a regular basis, yelping as if he had been stepped on, or simply barking into the darkness. Unlike us, I knew that he could see it. Animals are known to be able to see spirits that are invisible to humans. It became a regular occurrence to find him barking and growling at the doorways of seemingly empty rooms all over the house, especially the kitchen. On many occasions our cat would not enter the house when I opened the door to let her in. I would open the kitchen door and she would take one look, turn, and run off like she'd been hit with a dart, and sit at the edge of the yard looking back at the house. This became routine, as did all of the other tactics that the demon spirit used against all of us. We simply forced ourselves to go about our daily lives as best we could.

October was now upon us, the leaves were changing and falling from the trees, and I wasn't looking forward to another month of this Hell, especially if it was going to intensify as Fr. Ron indicated.

At least Bobby seemed to be settling down a little. One particular night I was gratified to find him kneeling beside his bed praying at two thirty in the morning. The smell of the stench was in his bedroom, and I commanded it to leave him alone.

Lesa continued to hear it moving furniture around on the second floor during the day, seemingly in a rage, as *The Passion* played in two rooms upstairs. Barb, the Christian mystic friend of Fr. Mike, told him that she had a vision that the spirit was focusing all of its energy now to break my resolve in a titanic effort—it was enraged that it had not succeeded and was more determined than ever to destroy me and drive my family out of the house. At this point after saying my nightly rosary aloud I also began to say in a strong voice the following prayer given to me by Fr. Ron to purify a house:

Spirit of our God, Father, Son, and Holy Spirit, Most Holy Trinity, Immaculate Virgin Mary, angels, archangels, and saints of Heaven, descend upon me . . . Please purify me Lord, fill me with yourself and use me . . . Banish all forces of evil from this house, destroy them, vanquish them, so that it can be a healthy and holy place to live.

Banish from this house all spells, witchcraft, black magic, malefic ties, maledictions, and the evil eye; diabolical infestations, oppressions, possessions; all that is evil and sinful, jealousy, perfidy, envy, physical, psychological, moral, spiritual, diabolic ailments . . . Burn all of these evils in Hell, that they may never again touch this house or any other person who lives in it . . .

I command and bid all of the powers who molest me, by the power of God all powerful, in the name of Jesus Christ our savior, through the intercession of the Immaculate Virgin Mary, to leave this house forever, and to be consigned into the everlasting Hell, where they will be bound by Saint Michael the Archangel, Saint Gabriel, Saint Raphael, our guardian angels, and where they will be crushed under the heel of the Immaculate Virgin Mary . . . Amen.

I would say this prayer so many times through the coming months that the words would flow from my mouth like water from a spring.

CHAPTER EIGHTEEN

The demon now began to harass me almost continuously when I was at home. One day I had to do some work on the sunporch that sits on the flat roof in the rear of the house off of the master bedroom, what was now the vacant sitting room. It was the middle of the day and I had to pass through that room and walk up three steps to exit onto the porch. The stench was strong in the room, and it followed me to the open door. I could feel it and smell it standing there. The thing was watching me.

I thought, "I don't have time for this nonsense now." When I came in I blessed the four corners of the room with holy water, set the rosary tape to play, closed the door to the room, and went downstairs to dinner. When I came back upstairs after dinner the room was clean of the stench and I finished my work.

That night Fr. Ron related a vision of the house surrounded by flames. I interpreted this as meaning we were now in the center of those flames. Fr. Ron told me to persevere and stay the course. That was somewhat easy for him to say because he didn't have to live here day to day. I was the one entering and living in "the Matrix." That night as Lesa and I had finished the rosary we came downstairs to find an extremely large puddle of the fluid (whatever it was) at the bottom of the steps.

A few days later I came home and found that I was alone in the house. I went directly to the second-floor sitting room, and, as it had been just about every day, the demon's stench was there waiting for me. I prayed from the Bible and as usual used different verses related to the sacrificial death of Jesus. I prayed for forgiveness for those who had been involved with what had happened in the house all those years ago. The stench grew even stronger.

Lesa came home and found me upstairs alone in the room. Without saying a word she put on the rosary tape and we began to pray in conjunction with it. We continued like this for over an hour as the thing moved around the room. It would seem to depart and then would return. I tried to follow it with a crucifix and the Bible in my two hands. This went on until Lesa had finally had enough of the stench, as it hung in the room like a suffocating smoke making it hard to breathe. I continued by myself for about another hour until I was too exhausted to go on. I left and the demon held the room. I had to retreat. It had won the day. It now seemed stronger than my will to confront it—and it was becoming more resilient.

I went downstairs and found Lesa on the phone with Fr. Ron, who had sensed that something critical was happening and had called the house a few minutes before. She gave me the phone.

"Bob, I know you're losing heart, but you must persevere in the battle," he said, knowing exactly what I needed to hear. "Don't give up. You have God on your side and you will win eventually. You must stay in the fight."

When I went back upstairs about a half hour later the room was clear. The following day I spoke with Fr. Mike and suggested that we take the battle to the demon once more and have Mass in the room that it was fighting to possess. We planned to do it when he was back in town in a few days. Two days later Fr. Mike came to the house in the afternoon. We met in the kitchen and reviewed the current state of affairs. Charlie was with us, and we hoped that his participation might help his state of mind, because the medication and psychiatric treatment didn't seem to be working.

The demonic stench kept moving all around that day. It was maddening. I had set up the altar in the main master bed/living room on the second floor in front of the fireplace—and when we entered we immediately noticed the presence of the stench. It wasn't strong, but nonetheless it was there. I didn't make an issue of it but just said, "It's here with us." Lesa looked at me and nodded in agreement.

I was astonished that the smell remained with us throughout the entire Mass, throughout the consecration, and as we received Holy Communion, but when we went downstairs after the Mass it was gone. Then it cleared from the room completely, possibly because I'd again turned up the sound on *The Passion* and the scourging scene was playing. Then

Lesa called up to me from the foyer that "it's down here now." But when I came downstairs it had vanished and all was calm. I knew that it was playing games with us, hitting us in new and different ways.

The next night, after returning home from an out-of-town meeting, I went directly upstairs. The stench was there and actually followed me into our bedroom. It occurred to me that this game was getting ridiculous. As I unpacked, I thought of a new tactic. I looked at where I thought the spirit was and began to laugh out loud and said, "You know something? You're a joke." Sure enough, the smell disappeared, as if the thing didn't know what to do.

A few days later I was watching television and came across a documentary that detailed various hauntings, including *The Amityville Horror*, which was rumored to be a hoax. I could easily relate to everything depicted, but it was nowhere near what we were going through. I also noted that in every instance the people involved were scared out of their wits and left in terror. We were experiencing months of relentless insanity, with no end in sight, and I thought that maybe I was crazy to stay, but at this point we were committed to the battle. I had faith in the power of Jesus and was convinced that in the end His holiness and righteousness could and would prevail.

The next day David told us that he was in his room listening to music when the volume began to go up and down on its own and then flashes of blue light began to appear over his bed. He calmly left the room and retrieved the rosary tape out of the central room, put it in his cassette player, turned it on, and left. No fuss or excitement; he had learned what to do.

It was now the first week of November, and five days of relative calm had passed, but I sensed that something new was soon coming. Sunday night arrived, and as I expected, the demon was back again in the same upstairs room waiting for me. Lesa and I went upstairs and entered the room, and I locked the door, signifying that we were not planning to leave.

"In the name of Jesus I command you to appear in this room so I can see you," I said forcefully and followed up with, "Tell me your name." I kept repeating the commands but nothing happened. However, the stench did grow weaker. To this point I had never actually seen the demon, unlike Bobby, Jessica, Tom, Collin, Lesa, and various visitors to the house. I wanted it to show itself to me so I could see exactly what I was fighting. I was sure the spirit was playing games with me—not showing itself was just another tactic.

I then pulled out a surprise. I read the Catholic rite of exorcism for a demon that was in possession of a particular place or locality. It was a lengthy ritual, and Lesa read the responsorial parts. This is generally only to be done by a priest, but by that time I was the guy on the ground and decided to use it anyway. Nothing dramatic happened, but when we were finished, surprisingly the spirit was gone and the room was clear and clean of its stench.

I went on to say the rosary later that night and again was surprised, if somewhat unsettled, by the resulting air of tranquility.

"Are you sure you don't miss fighting with the spirit,

Bob?" Fr. Ron commented when I spoke to him the next day.

"No, far from it, Father. I'll be the first one to celebrate when this battle is finally over. I only feel a bit wary of the calm. It's a welcome break, but I know the war has to continue, the storm is coming. I'd rather press the issue now," I said, using a military phrase.

During that first week of November when we were experiencing the lull in spiritual activity, I went downstairs one night to look for a board I'd found during the previous summer that had a name written on it. I thought it might provide a clue to what we were dealing with. I had told Fr. Ron about it, and he wanted to know what the name was.

I'd found the board when I was in the process of rebuilding a wall on the side of the small stone porch that was in back of the kitchen. While I was working I'd uncovered what appeared to be a small hidden room under it. As I pulled the stones away and found the large dark cavity I could smell the stale, nearly century-old air escaping. I called into the house and asked Lesa to get me a flashlight, and she came out and helped me pull the stones away to create a larger opening. As I looked into the darkness I was surprised to see what could have easily been a small room measuring approximately six feet by four feet. It was high enough for me to stand in, it had a dirt floor, and it looked as if the workman had just decided to wall it off rather than making a doorway to access it. The basement of the house is so large—and there was already a sizable dirt-floored fruit and vegetable cellar with storage racks—that the builder must have felt there was no need for another one. I made the opening large enough to crawl through and lowered myself down into it. To my surprise I found an old two-by-four about three feet long lying horizontally on the ground directly under the doorway that led into the kitchen. The wood felt almost like it had been freeze-dried; it was so light with no moisture in it at all. There was something written on it with what appeared to be white chalk. I handed it out to Lesa and crawled out to examine it in the light. It was a German name, and we determined that a workman had simply put it there for posterity.

I went inside and looked in the Pittsburgh phone book and couldn't find the name. It was getting dark by then, and eventually I just took the board downstairs to my workshop and leaned it against the wall, intending to research the name in the future. I didn't give it another thought and a few days later walled the room off again, placing a small time capsule of my own in the space.

On that November night, I went into the basement, and to my astonishment there was the board with the name on it, lying horizontally on the floor at the doorway to the furnace room. I hadn't paid any attention to the board since I had found it the previous summer. I'd actually forgotten all about it, and here it was lying across the doorway. I asked Lesa and the boys if they had placed it there, and they had no idea what I was talking about; no one had even been in the furnace room that day. Nor did the boys know anything about this board.

When I picked it up and looked at it to write down the name, it appeared as though something with a claw had picked every trace of the chalk writing off it. When I looked for wood chips on the floor there were none. No one in the house other than Lesa knew anything about the board or the name on it. It hadn't seemed to be all that significant, and I had simply set it aside and hadn't written the name down when I found it, which I regretted. By now Lesa and I had forgotten the name. Fr. Ron said he'd reflect on it nonetheless.

After some reflection, probably involving input from Connie, Fr. Ron told me the following story:

One of the construction workers had some romantic or sexual feelings for the young Mrs. Malick when the house was being built. She would come to visit the site dressed in fine clothes and a hat. Because she paid little mind to these lowly men of the working class he eventually began to refer to her as the "rich bitch" while working in the basement. He complained that she would have this big house while he and his family only had two small rooms to live in. This worker of European descent had possibly put a curse on the house, and this curse had something to do with this board I found under the back porch. The demon did not want me to tell Fr. Ron the name on the board, and that is why it was removed.

Fr. Ron then asked me if we had found a picture of the young Mrs. Malick somewhere in the house, and I told him that we had, that I couldn't remember exactly where we found it but that it was dated 1915 and she was in fact a very beautiful young woman.

Had she really played a part somehow in this curse cast on the house, and how might she be connected to what eventually occurred there?

CHAPTER NINETEEN

The same day I told Fr. Ron about the board incident we moved into another, even more ominous phase of our battle: We found what appeared to be a small puddle of red blood on the floor in the bathroom connected to our bedroom. We cleaned it up with a towel and bathroom cleaner, but the next morning the puddle had reappeared on the floor, and the bottle of cleaner that was still sitting on the floor next to the toilet was spotted with red blood as well. This was the beginning of a new, "bloody" phase of the demonic battle.

I also discovered that *The Passion* in the sitting room had been turned off completely, DVD player along with the television set. Lesa had come up with a brilliant idea to place her full-length freestanding mirror in front of the television so that it could be seen from every corner of the room. Apparently the thing didn't appreciate this and had turned the movie off.

I started finding little signs of its presence throughout the rooms. At night it would balance small items like pocket change and other ordinary objects standing on end in a way that communicated to me "I was here when you were asleep." It must have had an ironic sense of humor, because it took Dan Brown's book *Angels and Demons* that I was reading and painstakingly balanced it on end on top of a stuffed footstool in front of the chair in which I had been sitting the night before. (I would have had a hard time replicating the feat.) All of these acts were meant to unsettle me, and even though I didn't want to admit it, the thing was succeeding. I was weakening in my resolve and losing my confident state of mind. It was all around me.

As I cleaned up the blood for the second time, I spoke to it openly, with what I hoped was a confident tone: "In the name of Jesus, we are going to continue with this fight until you are expelled. On that you can rest assured. You are leaving; we are not."

Fr. Ron had specific instructions concerning the blood.

"You have to throw away any cloth that has come into contact with the fluid," he told me. "When you come across any blood, wipe it up with a paper towel, wrap it in a paper towel, and bury it near the rosebush in the backyard. Wipe your hands with holy water while also sprinkling holy water on the floor where it appeared."

"Are there angels in this house for our protection, Father?" By this time I felt the need for heavenly assistance.

"Yes, there are angels, Bob. You are being watched over by good as well as evil."

He explained that there is a hierarchical order that

governs angels and demons, and that angels can only do so much when dealing with the likes of a demon as powerful as the one in my house. The primary battle was still between my family and this demon, and the bulk of the struggle was focused upon me. He and the other priests, the rituals, and even the angels were there to support me, but I had been preordained long ago by God to fight this battle.

By now these thoughts no longer fed my ego as they once had; I wanted to be finished with this insanity and go back to leading a normal life. I was tired and wasn't sure that I had the stamina to continue. But I was angry, and this anger fueled my confidence that we could ultimately prevail through the power of another type of blood, the blood of Jesus. Like the old-time Baptist gospel hymn I used to sing with the kids, "There Is Power in the Blood"! Lord, I needed that power now.

"How can we sleep, or even worse, make love in our bedroom when it's leaving puddles of blood on the bathroom floor?" I asked Father one day.

"It's extremely important to continue to live as normally as possible while this is going on, Bob," Fr. Ron told me. "The demon wants to upset you and cause dissension."

"What do you mean normal, Father? How can we possibly pretend things are normal?"

"I mean that your sexual relations should continue unabated and as often as practical. The natural love between a husband and a wife is a powerful tool against evil, which can't stand such natural relations as designed by God."

It seemed a little strange to talk about having a lot of sex with all that was going on, but he explained that this is why evil does its best to pervert what was designed by God to be a holy act.

"But Father, the notion of making love with a demon watching us is pretty weird."

"You and Lesa making love is actually a weapon against the Devil, Bob," Fr. Ron reassured me. "Don't worry about it watching you—it simply can't."

This advice certainly sounded great to me, right up my alley!

I told Lesa, "Okay, this is the plan: sex and a lot of it, every day, for the good of the cause!"

"Oh, I'm sure Father really emphasized it exactly like that," she responded, smiling.

We were happy to comply.

On Thanksgiving Day Bobby called me into the central room and showed me a new phenomenon concerning the blood. In the central bedroom/living room there is a ceiling fan with three Victorian-style lamps that hang under the fan. One of the bulbs had burned out, and he showed me how all three had what appeared to be red blood that had run down from the metal bulb threads to form drops—which had dried—at the center base of each bulb. The bulbs were round and milky white. It is also interesting to note that all three were eventually found broken at different times in the future when I had set them aside to show Fr. Mike.

The most worrisome problem was still Charlie. His cutting especially had gotten more severe and coincided with the demon depositing bloody puddles in our bathroom.

We were very concerned and talked about moving him into Jessica's house, but he refused.

At this point Fr. Ron told me that we could expect a "time of peace" in the house as the holidays approached but that things would become very intense and begin again in January. This was certainly good news to hear for a change, and just as he said, not long after Thanksgiving, as Lesa began to decorate the house for Christmas, all of the paranormal activity stopped. Charlie was beginning to settle down as well now that he was getting new therapy and was enrolled in a special school for teenagers with emotional difficulties. His anxiety attacks were abating, and Bobby was doing better, too. His wild rages had stopped as he was also becoming more engaged in what was happening in the house. Things seemed almost normal for the first time in months. Fr. Ron advised that we should have Mass in the house around Christmas week and that we should all enjoy the peace and prepare ourselves mentally and spiritually for the onslaught that was coming after the first of the New Year.

The Bible tells us, "Submit to God, resist the Devil and he will flee from you. Draw near to God and He will draw near to you." I believed these words and was putting my family through Hell in the process. A moment of truth for my faith was near. It was one thing for me to be willing to fight this fight, but the people I loved most were becoming serious casualties in the process, again just like with the evil in Brentwood. I had mixed feelings about moving them out of the house. I didn't want to send a signal that we were giving in and retreating. Moving Collin out was one thing, because he was helpless and had no idea what was going on. On the other hand, Lesa and the boys had faith that I knew what I was doing and also drew their strength from me. I just had to trust that I did in fact know what I was doing and could maintain my strength, and faith, to continue to resist this heinous thing. If the demon was pushing back hard that meant it was being hit hard. It was paradoxical, but I knew that we were making progress by the strength of its attacks. We had to stand firm and trust in those words "resist the Devil and he will flee from you." Eventually.

As Fr. Ron advised, we celebrated Mass in the living room of the house on December 30, 2004. But our resolve was about to be undermined by internal dissension once again.

Things had been calm through Christmas as far as the demon was concerned, but Lesa and I weren't speaking and I was extremely upset with her. On Christmas Eve I had discovered that she had secretly been spending thousands of dollars over our budget on Christmas gifts and other things for months. It caught me completely by surprise. All of a sudden I had stumbled onto the fact that I owed over twenty thousand dollars on a credit card I didn't know she had! She said that she did it because of all of the turmoil, but it only brought back many bad memories for me of her issues eight years earlier. Fr. Ron counseled us that we should do our best to reconcile because the demon drew its energy from family dissension. In some devious manner I believed that it had planned this to coincide with the attack that it would soon unleash and was doing its best to weaken me. I could see that and it was working. All of my pent-up emotions from being arrested and put out of the house in 2003 came crashing back down on me. I was suddenly greatly tempted to walk out of the picture, give up, and leave. One part of my mind knew exactly what was happening, but my emotions were extremely difficult to control. How much more could be dumped on my shoulders?

Fr. Ron did his best to keep me focused, but inside I was falling apart under the pressure. I was ready to give up. I just couldn't take it anymore. Fr. Mike spent time with Lesa and the boys, who were struggling now because of me. All seemed to be lost, and these priests were doing their best to hold our family together. I wanted out and even talked to my attorney about divorce.

The night of the Mass I found the St. Benedict's crucifix that I had attached to the pull chain on the closet light wrapped around the light. I felt like I was going backward. It was extremely demoralizing.

Fr. Ron called the next day to tell me that one of his visions had revealed Mrs. Malick looking out of the blue room on the second floor not long after she had gone through an abortion procedure performed by the doctor to terminate the pregnancy of a third child. He said that the doctor had given her a thick black substance to drink during the procedure. He also said that possibly the graves of some young children were disturbed when the foundation for the house was excavated in 1909. These children were not related to the Malicks or the abortion doctor. I would later find out more details about who they were and how they died. At the time I didn't know what any of this meant, but it certainly wasn't good news. Somehow I had to pull myself together and resist the mental attack of this evil entity.

During the first two weeks of January I tried to get my head on straight but I wasn't able to. The thing had me in such a weakened state that it soon would be pushing us out the door. I knew that if I left it would win. It had driven me out once before and was on the verge of doing it again.

I didn't have any time to recover, because on the thirteenth of January the demon began its anticipated grand attack. Since Jessica and her family had moved out, the third floor was vacant and I had been retreating to it and actually sleeping there for solitude. Moving to the third floor was the first step in moving out. My mind was a mess. I also had contracted the flu and was pretty sick. I came home early that afternoon to go to bed; no one was home and the house was empty. As I walked up the steps to the third floor I was struck with an unbelievable sight at the top of the stairs.

All of the walls including two doors were spattered with large drops of red blood from the ceiling to the floor. The blood was still wet and was running down the walls. It was as if someone had just taken a container and a sponge and sprinkled the walls as Fr. Mike had done numerous times with holy water.

After I realized what I was looking at I went downstairs and called Fr. Ron.

"This is just the type of thing I expected, Bob. Don't be alarmed."

That was easy for him to say, but he didn't have to look at blood dripping down the walls. Lesa soon came home and I showed her the ghastly discovery. We didn't touch it except for a small area that I had originally wiped with a towel just to see what it was.

Over the next several weeks the blood continued to be sprinkled down both staircases to the first floor, including my den. Some of the areas where the blood was dripping from were so far up (nine feet) that a person would have had to use a ladder to get there. Another interesting aspect was that it was only on the walls and not on the ceilings so that if it were thrown up there it would have been impossible to miss hitting the ceilings. It looked as if the walls were bleeding.

"This is the demon's way of claiming the house for evil—with its stench and the blood of death—just as we had claimed the house for good with holy water and blessed incense," Fr. Ron explained.

"This thing seems to be taunting me and openly claiming victory," I said, feeling unsure of what my next step should be.

"It depends on the way you look at it. I see it as reacting to your assaults with ever greater attempts at intimidation. Just remember to keep repeating your prayer: "This is my house, this is my family. You are going to leave in the name of Jesus." I did know that when I used that prayer the words gave me strength.

The following morning Fr. Mike and Kerry came by the house to look at the spectacle. I took samples of the wet substances on Q-tips and also took pictures of it. I later discovered that the inside lining of the lampshade on my nightstand was spattered with blood as well. Fr. Mike prayed to bind the spirit from any further activity, but the walls kept bleeding unabated.

The blood on the walls had the opposite effect as intended. It didn't demoralize me as much as shocked me to my senses. I might have been down for the count, but this event energized me to get up to continue the fight. I now had a clear head again, even though it had made its big move. Lesa and I reconciled and I conquered my emotions. As Rocky Balboa said: "Life isn't about how hard you can hit . . . it's about how hard you can get hit and keep moving forward." This fight certainly wasn't over yet.

PART THREE

CHAPTER TWENTY

At this point Fr. Ron advised me to take an unusual step. He gave me the website address of a group of researchers affiliated with Pennsylvania State University. The group was called the Penn State Paranormal Research Society.

"It's time to document what's happening in the house by an organization apart from the diocese."

"Why? What do you have in mind, Father?"

"If we're going to go for a real exorcism, the Church requires examination and verification by professionals apart from the Church," he explained.

"I thought that was just in the case of a possession of a person?"

"No, it includes the infestation of a house as well."

"Hasn't Fr. Mike been exorcising the house?" I asked.

"He can't; he's not an exorcist. He's a priest and is only allowed to say deliverance prayers. An exorcism has to be performed by a priest trained specifically in that ritual. And the Church requires outside verification of demonic infestation in order to send an exorcist. It's a significant step, and not done casually."

That evening I composed the following e-mail:

To whom it may concern:

My name is Bob Cranmer and my family and I live in Pittsburgh. To start with I am not a nut or a prankster. I am an executive with a well known engineering firm and was formerly the chairman of the board of county commissioners in Allegheny County. I was told this evening by a highly placed priest of the Catholic Diocese of Pittsburgh to contact you. For the past year we have been engaged in what has amounted to a "battle" with an evil spirit in our home. There have been three priests working with us continuously and the things that we have experienced I would not believe had I not experienced them first hand.

I have kept a record of all of the events as they have happened. For the past two months things have been relatively quiet. One of the priests who we work with (who is a mystic) predicted that the manifestations would stop through the holidays but would begin again in earnest this month. Tonight I came home from work to find the walls of a stairway which leads to the third floor (this is an old house) covered with droplets of blood.

At first I thought that someone had splashed something on the wall until I looked and saw the wallpaper was covered all the way up to the ceiling out of my reach, and

I'm six feet tall. In the past months we've also experienced small puddles of blood in one of the bathrooms and larger puddles of a clear substance that appeared in the hallways of both the first and second floors.

A "figure dressed in black" has been seen by my children, my wife, and I have been directly in its presence as well. In the past months it has given off a "stench" similar to burning rubber and has moved around a particular bedroom. It generally always reacts to the priests when they are here and it certainly doesn't like Mass to be celebrated in the house either.

I could go on in great detail and at length. Up to this point it has been a private matter and I have only interacted with the priests. Tonight I was advised by one of them to contact you. I am doing so reluctantly for I am not seeking any attention or publicity. Being a public figure I am aware of what the media would do with a story like this. I believe that my wife and two of my sons have been affected mentally by this thing, and my little 3 year old grandson was accosted by it one afternoon last summer.

If you are interested in any way you can call or e-mail me, but I want no publicity.

Bob Cranmer
Pittsburgh, PA

The next day I received a phone call from Ryan Buell, the group's leader. He indicated that he would like to speak with me over the weekend in greater detail. I thanked him and we agreed that he would call me on

Saturday, but I did not hear from him. I was disappointed and hoped that he hadn't written me off. But I then received an e-mail in which he apologized for not getting in touch over the weekend. He asked me when I would be available for an interview.

At this point a rift began to appear between Fr. Ron and Fr. Mike. Fr. Ron was looking for outside verification of the spiritual phenomenon taking place in the house, but Fr. Mike was concerned that anything taking place in the house should be purely Christian in nature, and in no way psychological or academic. He felt that a secular scientific validation would serve no purpose whatsoever in the expulsion efforts. I told him that I agreed with Fr. Ron and that this group might help us to better understand the power and tactics of the demon. Ultimately I didn't see how the activity of these researchers could hinder our efforts. He reluctantly agreed but would not be available for their initial visit to the house. This was his protest, and I was disappointed, as I considered us a team.

I had several in-depth informal interviews with Ryan over the phone during the next week and told him the blood on the doors had not soaked in as it had done on the wallpaper and that the drops were dried and clearly visible. He wanted to speak with the priests involved and said that he planned to bring a group of eight to ten people to the house. This startled me a little. At that point I didn't realize that he was more the leader of a "campus club" of students rather than the head of an organized research team of experts. Of course he and his group would later become the stars of the hit TV show *Paranormal State*.

Ryan said that he was a Catholic and that several others in his group were as well. They did in fact make prayer part of their work, and they also utilized the gifts of a well-known psychic from Gettysburg named Julie, who was Catholic and had been involved with demons before. Initially she was going to accompany them, however at the last minute said that she couldn't or wouldn't. But their work was primarily scientific, utilizing recorders, video cameras, temperature devices, and other technical, scientific instruments.

Fr. Ron did not particularly want to converse with or reveal himself to them. He said it would be more appropriate for Fr. Mike to be the priest on the ground, so to speak. I found myself in an interesting dilemma and simply decided to move forward with this group on my own and play it by ear as things unfolded. If this group could help me to learn how to flush this thing out into the open, all the better. It had been stalking us so far, but if they could show me how to stalk it in return, the battle could then truly be fought on even terms. I wanted to discover where it retreated to in the house during periods of inactivity, if it did, in fact, retreat, so as to possibly follow it there. Up to this point it chose when and where confrontations would take place. If we could discover its lair we might be able to prevent it from getting the rest and recuperation it seemed to require.

The visit of the PRS group was set for the following weekend in late January. Julie, the psychic from

Gettysburg, who would not be coming with the group but had apparently already related to them some pertinent information regarding the house. Fr. Ron also agreed to speak with Ryan by phone since Fr. Mike was not available. I believed that this was by design, and apparently Fr. Ron had come to the same conclusion. This rift would continue to grow over the coming month and eventually threatened to undermine the effectiveness of our close-knit team, a development that I came to believe was perpetrated by the demon. I would have to attempt to keep this rift from destroying our progress and would work hard to keep us all united.

In the days prior to the PRS group's arrival the activity in the house increased. The bumping of furniture being moved and knocking on the walls intensified while a gold metal cross that Charlie had been wearing disappeared from around his neck while he was sleeping. We later searched and found it in his room bent and folded in half upon itself.

In addition, cold spots began to emerge at various places in the house. This was a new phenomenon. It felt like you were walking past an open window in those areas. Fr. Ron spoke to Ryan on Thursday night, the day before the team was scheduled to arrive. All was set for a very interesting weekend to come.

Ryan and his team did not arrive until almost 11:00 P.M. Friday night. They drove in several cars from State College, Pennsylvania, and two others came all the way from New Haven, Connecticut. They were all students in their early to mid-twenties, except for Adam Blai, who was an instructor and advisor to the team. Ryan was a

slim, handsome young man who even then had the flair
and dramatic presence that eventually landed him a TV
show. Adam was a serious, balding, conservatively dressed
man in his thirties with an air of gravity—the scholar of
the team. He had an encyclopedic knowledge of demonology and would later leave the flamboyant PRS team
and become a consultant to the Catholic Church on the
subject.

Despite their youth, the group was extremely professional and came into the house like the A-Team. They
set up a headquarters of sorts on the third floor and then
began to strategically place instruments to monitor temperature on each of the four floors, a wireless network
for their computer and Internet communications, video
cameras, handheld cameras and communication devices,
electromagnetic pulse measuring devices, tape recorders, temperature recorders, infrared cameras, and other
impressive-looking equipment. These young people were
all business and took their work very seriously. We were
impressed. They conducted a meeting, went to work,
and told us that we could go to bed for the night. By
then it was 2:30 A.M. We did just that, and I was confident that they knew exactly what they were doing.

Nothing of any major significance happened that night,
but they reported in the morning that their instruments
had detected various readings of paranormal activity in the
house. The next day they reported to me that their psychic, Julie, had told them that there was a hidden spot in
the center of the house that they should seek to uncover. I
told them that there was in fact such a space and that I had
always wondered about it as well but had never attempted

to access it. The space was the area behind the walk-in coat closet with the pull-chain light where activity had gone on for years. It was under the large wooden staircase leading to the second floor. I showed them the spot, and Ryan recommended that we break into it. This was no simple task. I would have to cut through plaster wall and lath boards in the back of the closet, into an area that measured approximately three feet by five feet by four feet in dimension, tapering off in the shape of an "L". I brought up the required power and hand tools from the basement and went to work. It took about a half hour to cut a hole big enough to pass through, and I was surprised how large a space it was once we did.

The area was about four and a half feet in height and was filled with black coal dust. There were some extremely small cracks between the floorboards, but otherwise it was completely sealed off. The air was musty, and I knew that this area had been closed since 1910 when the house was built. I looked into the space with a flashlight and saw nothing of significance. Kerry had arrived by this point, and we watched as Adam and Ryan donned breathing respirators and head-mounted lights and entered the space to investigate it. They spent over an hour in the space, and we were astonished with the items that they found.

In the center of the floor they discovered an amber stone, large enough to cover the palm of my hand. I later read that the belief that amber warded off evil spirits dated to pre-Roman times. It is the fossilized resin of ancient trees. Most of the world's amber is believed to be 30 to 90 million years old. Amber pendants were worn throughout Europe to preserve chastity, and also used to make rosary beads to guard against evil. Amber would be burned with frankincense, myrrh, and copal to dispel evil spirits. Was this piece of amber taken at some point by the demon? I can only speculate how it made its way into this closed-off space with the other items found.

The team also found the complete skeleton of a small bird and three playing cards: the king of spades from one deck and the queen and three of hearts from another deck. (An interesting item that I learned was that the house was used for years by a local women's bridge club during the 1920s. This same group may have possibly held séances, which was a popular recreational activity of that era.)

But by far the two items found that brought the most attention were a Lego toy that came from a large collection my son Charlie had as a child and hand-drawn pictures on a piece of crumpled paper.

On one side of the paper there seemed to be a depiction of the view from the backyard of the house at sunset. It was a sketch of two pretty female faces smiling and gazing up at the sunset, one older, one younger, with birds in the sky along with large trees in the background and a picket fence in the foreground. It was signed "H.P. Malick." The initials AMB also appeared on the picture, an obviously pleasant, happy family scene. The other side had a sketch of a man's face with a big nose and a cigar in his mouth, a pig's head, a man laughing at him behind his back, and a snake coiled ready to bite the man. Most interesting, the edges seemed to be scorched, and it was not folded, but crumpled up in a ball. Why would it be in this closed space? Was the pleasant family scene meant to be cursed by the evil depictions on the back and then discarded here?

Connie Valenti later said the paper was supposed to have been crumpled up and burned as a *malocchio*, or curse, cast possibly by a workman, which would condemn the house to burn, and in fact a serious fire did once occur on the third floor. The *malocchio* is the belief in the evil eye, placed on a person when someone else is jealous or envious of the other's good luck. The *malocchio* then manifests itself in some sort of misfortune for the cursed person or persons. This workman had more than a few reasons to envy and resent Malick. For one he had a beautiful wife, and another reason, according to Connie, was that Malick owed him money that he didn't pay. Possibly the workman took a piece of paper already signed by Malick and used his name to cast his curse. Actually both forms of his name were on the paper—his printed name and his signature. She also said that several "accidents" occurred during the construction of the house and that one of the workmen had walked off the job claiming that the ground itself was "cursed by evil."

The biggest mystery was how the Lego toy got in there. This area was completely closed off with no access whatsoever other than the tiny floorboard cracks that let the coal dust in from the basement below. Were these items that the spirit had taken through the years from occupants of the house for some unknown reason? Was the Lego used in some way to harm Charlie? It seemed as though we had found the space we had been looking for.

Finding the demon's lair made things real in a way they never had been before. I began to analyze the spirit rationally. One, even though it was supernatural and had the powers to pass through walls with unlimited movement and take on different forms, it was still an entity and had to be limited to a single place in the house; that is, it couldn't be in the basement and on the third floor at the same time. Two, if it was in the house at all times, it had to have a resting spot, and if it wasn't bothering us it was curled up somewhere doing whatever it did during its downtime. Three, it did have supernatural powers, but there were obviously limits to these powers. It could attempt to terrorize us with demonstrations that defied rational explanations—like the blood and the stench—and it could attack us mentally and physically, but only to an extent. If it could kill us or do extreme bodily harm, it obviously would have done that by now. There were limits to what it was capable of doing, and resisting it was still obviously within the realm of our human abilities.

On the other hand, our means of resisting crossed over into the supernatural as well. How and to what extent I didn't fully understand, but it didn't mangle the crosses, interconnect the rosaries, and flee from the holy water and holy incense for nothing. Like a rifle can be a lethal instrument when aimed correctly, the same can be said for holy weapons. I used them without fully understanding how and why they worked, but I knew they were powerful and caused this thing pain.

We apparently also had supernatural forces of good around us as well. How many angels were involved I could never know, but they were obviously present, and probably were there to place limits on this thing's power, preventing it from simply killing us at will. Their role might be to keep the battle fair, but apparently they could not fight it for us. By cutting into the space under the steps we had invaded its territory and apparently had found its lair, its home. And just like any dragon, it undoubtedly wasn't too happy about it. We had struck a blow, and the hunter was now the hunted for a change. What this meant, or how it would be affected, I didn't know, but I did realize that this attack had to be pushed forward. Being a military historian I've always been an admirer of Stonewall Jackson, whose primary military maxim was:

> *Always mystify, mislead, and surprise the enemy if possible; and when you strike and overcome him, never let up in the pursuit . . . Never fight against heavy odds, if by maneuvering you can hurl your force on the weakest part of your enemy. Such tactics will win every time, and a smaller army may thus destroy a large one in detail, and repeated victory will make it invincible.*

We had an arsenal of weapons; we simply had to use them correctly and in force, at the right time and place for as long as it took.

By the time we cleaned up and recorded what had taken place it was late in the afternoon. I told the group that I would take them all out to dinner and that we would leave the house empty to see if anything would be recorded on their instruments while we were gone. We had a delightful time at dinner, but when we came home after about two hours of the house being empty, it had a strange ominous and oppressive feel that is hard to describe, like a town in which an angry mob is preparing to riot. Anger and rage filled the air.

Within a few minutes Fr. Ron called.

"Is everything alright? I've been picking up extreme anger, cursing, and agitation emanating from your house."

"Everything is fine right now, Father. The team is preparing for a night of observation and instrument monitoring."

"Please be careful, and tell them the same. I'll call again."

Then one of the team member's cell phones rang and it was Julie, the psychic from Gettysburg who had told us to find the hidden space.

She asked to speak to Adam and told him, "There are powerful feelings of anger coming from the house. I'm very concerned for the team's safety."

He told her that we would proceed very carefully. Ryan and Adam then assembled their team and related to them what we'd heard from Julie and Fr. Ron. I thought it was quite amazing that they both picked up the same feelings at the same time in towns almost two hundred miles apart.

The team took to their various stations throughout the house and waited for something to happen. I was calm about the situation and felt satisfied that after months of battling this thing, it had finally taken a punch that sent it to the canvas. It had done its best to take the master bedroom on the second floor away from me, but now I had entered into its space, and that felt good. The battle wasn't over by a long shot, but at this time, on this day, for this round, the evil spirit was the one surprised, dominated, and knocked down. I now knew I had gained strength and the confidence to continue. It could be hurt.

I went to bed around midnight, but Lesa stayed up with the team, as the tension was high in the house and she was familiar with the thing and knew that the team might need assistance as the night wore on. Around 4:00 A.M. the team gathered for a meeting and prayer session of sorts in the first-floor library, with two of them standing guard outside of the closed doors. A few of them said that the feelings and readings that they were getting were really starting to scare them. Lesa told me that one of them went into a trance and began to talk of the spirits of "children" being held captive in the house along with the spirit of "an old woman" (possibly my aunt who had died in the house). That group member then said that several angels appeared and swept these captive spirits away while the weakened, angry demon was forced to watch from a distance.

Adam Blai's verbal account of that night:

> Ryan and six or seven people were praying in Bob's library. We didn't know what was going on with the case at that time. Ryan had a camcorder on a tripod in the back of the room.
>
> This next part I don't talk about much in public, but after being exposed to this stuff for years I've developed a lot of sensitivity. As we were praying, in my mind's eye I felt very strongly that under the stairs it felt like a deformed or abused child was coming toward the room even though the door was closed. It felt sad and upset like it was coming towards the prayer wanting help. I felt like there was something wrong, then a really strong evil presence came into the room and everyone

*felt it, they kind of rocked back on their heels. We were in
a circle and we leaned back, repulsed by it. In my mind's
eye I saw and almost heard this mocking, evil, really
arrogant thing floating up there in the room maybe
four feet off the floor and I saw that it had babies
wrapped around it. It was disgusting, it was male and
it seemed to come when that child was coming for help.
It was worse than repulsive.*

*There was a camcorder running at the back of the
room and we didn't know it at the time but it went
black right before that evil presence came into the room.
We were kind of freaked out so we said the St. Michael
prayer and then it did feel like positive forces came into
the room.*

Exhausted, the team disbanded and went to the third
floor to sleep. The next day when this was all related to
me, I didn't know what to make of it, but the house did
seem much calmer. The team slept until early afternoon,
and we talked for some time once they reassembled. I
could tell that these young people had been moved and
startled by their experiences during those early morning
hours. Lesa prepared dinner, and they packed up their
equipment and left the house around 7:00 P.M. These
ghost-busters seemed to be busted themselves but had
done quite a job in the process.

During the weekend we talked about the similarity of
the names associated with the house. I noted how similar the name of the first owners, Malick, was to a notorious name in the Bible. Moloch was the chief god of the
Phoenicians and Canaanites. Babies were slowly burned

to death in the arms of the metal idol that was heated from the inside as a sacrifice to Moloch. The remains would burn and were apparently placed into small pots to be buried, as hundreds of these pots have been discovered. With all of the deaths that took place in the house, the similarity between the family name and the idol is hard to ignore. Another odd similarity is that *malocchio* is close to Moloch, and when I looked it up I found that another word for *malocchio* is, in fact, *maloik*.

The house had been marked by the Pittsburgh History and Landmarks Foundation with a brass plaque that labeled it as "The Malick House." I later removed this plaque and had a new one made with a different name: "Grand Oaks Manor," after the two centuries-old oak trees in the front yard. I took the Malick plaque and put it in the wood furnace to hold the hot coals of the burning wood on the large grates. It is still there, warped and melted, hardly distinguishable. I thought that burning it was a fitting fate in light of what had been perpetrated in this house so many years before.

CHAPTER TWENTY-ONE

During the first week of February Fr. Mike came to the house and celebrated Mass on the third floor where the heaviest amount of blood had been dripping down the walls. Kerry attended as well. Fr. Ron asked that Fr. Mike also bless the wall in the TV room that enclosed the door of sorrows and the area under the steps with holy water. Charlie had a very difficult time that week with his counselor and was taken directly from her office to the local hospital for observation. He was starting to come apart emotionally again and was suffering extreme anxiety attacks.

To take a break, Lesa and I booked two nights the next weekend at a small bed-and-breakfast about fifty miles north of Pittsburgh in Slippery Rock, Pennsylvania. After we arrived at the B and B that evening she unexpectedly became so ill that I thought that I was going to have to take her to the local hospital. The following day we returned home. She got some antibiotics and felt better, but the illness came out of nowhere very quickly. It seems the demon didn't want us to have any R and R from this battlefield.

That Sunday afternoon, as she was recovering, I went in to further clean up the closet where I had cut out the wall the previous week and also clean out the new open space beneath the steps for storage. It eventually would be a convenient space for all of our Christmas decorations. I decided to enlarge the opening and replaster the outer edges where I had cut it, replace a shelf, and generally make it look presentable again. However, to my dismay, even though it was a relatively simple job, I became overwhelmed with anger and agitation while I was in the closet. I couldn't understand where the feelings were coming from, since they weren't directed at anyone or anything in particular. I continued working, and as I began to scrub down the space with soap and water the feelings dissipated a little, but later they returned until I left the enclosed space. After I cleaned the space thoroughly with hot, soapy water, I installed an electric light and played the rosary tape several times as well.

The oppressive feeling in the house didn't disappear for long. The familiar, ominous, heavy, menacing aura soon returned. One day I noticed our dog staring off into space a number of times as if he were watching the evil spirit, as though hypnotized by it. I looked directly into the kitchen where the dog was fixated and commanded the thing in the name of Jesus to appear before me. Unexpectedly and suddenly my eyesight became blurred and I thought finally I'd see the thing but nothing appeared.

Lesa had a phone conversation with Julie that week and was told that her unexpected illness was caused by the demon and so was the latest round of Charlie's anxiety-fueled behavior. The demon's will was to break up our marriage along with our family and thereby force us to eventually leave the house, but we knew that already. Fr. Ron added that Charlie had experienced something extremely frightening in the house when he was very young, and even though he was able to effectively block it out, it was still there haunting his subconscious.

Meanwhile Ryan and his PRS team were anxious to come back to the house. From the excitement he exhibited in his e-mails to me I got the impression that this was the first significant case these young researchers had come across and he wanted to make the most of it. They must have felt they'd hit the mother lode of paranormal activity.

At the same time, the team I had assembled was beginning to turn on itself. The conflict had originated with Fr. Mike and his desire to control the deliverance process. I thought it simply had its origins in the different standings Fr. Ron and Fr. Mike held in the hierarchy of the local dioceses. Fr. Ron was high up and had been assigned by Bishop Wuerl to work with me. Fr. Mike, on the other hand, well known for his work with the Passionist order, was viewed as a "wildcatter" because of his close association with Pentecostal Protestants. He was involved with the early Catholic charismatic movement at Duquesne University of the Holy Spirit in Pittsburgh, regularly prayed in tongues, and certainly was not your average

Catholic priest. Even though I was never a charismatic Christian and have never prayed or spoken in tongues, I in no way saw this as a detriment to our effort. Quite the contrary, I viewed it as a unique qualification for a unique situation, giving strength to our cause. But I always sensed that there was a wall between Fr. Mike and Fr. Ron that prevented open cooperation. Fr. Ron could be compared to a federal marshall while Fr. Mike was the independent good-guy gunslinger. They rarely spoke to each other as far as I knew. I was the conduit between them. I believe that Fr. Mike wanted the diocese to embrace his rather unorthodox techniques and views, which wasn't going to happen. But he was determined nonetheless to get the Church to view these cases as a growing problem and not just as isolated incidents.

To further complicate the situation, Fr. Mike expressed consternation about the PRS team coming back to the house for another visit. He wasn't pleased with Fr. Ron asking me to contact PRS to begin with and said that any efforts to engage the demon in a secular manner could be very detrimental. I didn't fully disagree with him, but Fr. Ron and I both viewed their involvement as being one solely of outside verification. In spite of being surprised and somewhat concerned with their prayer-circle exercise, I did want PRS to return. Fr. Mike suggested that we put it off, but I disagreed, sensing an opportunity to make progress. Again, I wanted to press the issue . . . never let up in the pursuit. I thought that if they could flush the thing out again in a weakened state with Fr. Mike present, we could be waiting there to confront it spiritually on our own terms. Fr. Mike finally agreed, and to address his concerns I sent the following message to PRS to clarify the situation:

2/14/05

Ryan:

I believe that PRS can play an important role of validating (from a non-religious—scientific perspective), that something is, and has been, in fact going on in our home. I did not feel that your group would play a role in the deliverance process, and was surprised when you brought a spiritual perspective, as well as a scientific one along with you. The whole exercise of cutting into the steps, and what we found as a result was credible enough for me and it also added to insight that had already been provided to me by Fr. Ron some months earlier.

At this point I think that it is important to draw a line between your group and the Church. Fr. Mike and Fr. Ron are playing key spiritual roles in this battle and it is important that we don't blur the expertise here, so to speak. I view the purpose of your group primarily as outside validation. We have to coordinate our activities on this end a little better as well.

Your role as I see it:

1. Validate that there is serious paranormal activity in the house.

2. Provide advice as how to live with these entities as long as they are present.

3. Validate and/or support what we already have discerned.

4. Document this case to the best of your ability.

I want to prevent the group from falling into disarray over who's doing what.

Give me an idea of what you had planned to do this weekend and we can discuss, by phone if you like.

Thanks,
Bob Cranmer

I had to keep the peace because Fr. Mike was so very important to the process and had been at my side almost from the beginning. One bright spot was that Fr. Mike did seem to have some interest in working with Adam Blai of the PRS group because he was a devout Catholic and identified with his concerns. However, I had to marshal these forces for a coordinated attack. This evil thing was angry, looking for a fight, and I didn't want internal discord to get in the way of our giving it one.

As all of this activity played out, the battle still remained between me and the demon. It had focused its efforts upon weakening and ultimately crushing me, and I was the one who had been sent here to direct the forces of good to crush and expel it. Fr. Ron repeated this to me on a regular basis while I continued my daily prayers, rosary, and kept *The Passion* playing twenty-four hours a day in the blue room on the second floor. I placed a Bible and a crucifix in the space under the steps and regularly prayed and read scripture aloud there as well.

Once all of this was settled, PRS was scheduled to return, and I had gained the cooperation of Fr. Mike, Fr. Ron called me with more information.

"Bob, you're going to find a valuable diamond ring in the house. The doctor would sometimes accept jewelry as payment for his services. When you find it, no one should put it on their finger, as it has already had two owners."

I had no idea what this meant, but sure enough, a few months later Bobby found the ring in a space on the third floor. (I still have it, and it won't be worn. We've found a blue sapphire ring as well.)

"The main bathroom on the second floor should be monitored by PRS," Fr. Ron added. "The blood of the women the doctor injured was washed down a bathtub with claw-type feet."

"There's no claw-foot tub anymore, Father. That bathroom was modernized at some point and it now has a raised floor and a newer tub that looks to date to the 1940s."

"How about the bedroom with green wallpaper with flowers?"

"There is a room with green wallpaper with plants and leaves on it."

"That's close enough. I hear sounds of moaning and whispers coming from the room, but they're not from the demon. If you hear sounds in this room, say, 'Go in peace toward the light.' "

"That's the room where my aunt died, Father. I'll make sure I do it. I'd hate for her to be trapped here."

"Also, I think a worker was killed in an accident at the mill where the wood for the house was being cut and that some of his blood splashed onto the wood and is still there."

"Where is the wood in the house now, Father?"

"I'm not sure. I'll get back to you on that. May you have a gentle and joy-filled day."

The PRS team arrived around 8:00 P.M. on Friday, February 21, 2005, and it would prove to be an eventful visit. They set up their equipment and once again used the third floor as a base. We let them work and went to bed around midnight. As they were having a meeting on the third floor, sometime early in the morning hours, three very pronounced scratches suddenly appeared horizontally across Adam's forehead. This was caught on tape, and when I saw them the next morning I told them that they were the exact same scratches that had appeared numerous times on my neck and chest. However, blood actually ran down Adam's forehead. Also, what was different about this incident was that Adam was not asleep when it occurred, and others actually saw it happen.

Adam later related his story of the night:

It was cold, and snowing outside. We were talking on the third floor but it felt oppressive and overwhelming. I walked outside with Ryan and Elfie, one of the girls in the class, to breathe. We walked for about fifteen to twenty minutes. Then lightning hit nearby and everything went black except the four streetlights right around us. We felt like we needed to get back right away because something may have gone wrong.

We returned to the apartment on the top floor and entered one of the crawl spaces off the back room. Ryan demanded that the demon say its name. We were sitting in tight quarters when he said, "I demand you to say your name." My eyes were open but I saw letters as if there was a piece of paper held in front of me, I saw "S" "A" "T." The next letter was "H." We left the crawl space and when I got home I looked for names and turns out that Sathi is a female demon.

Then everyone was brainstorming about what do we do, what does it mean? I was very new to all of this and hadn't had these strange images and impressions before. I thought maybe I should reflect on it. I went to the other room alone, sat on the floor, closed my eyes, meditated, I pictured the house and I could see it. Underneath the lower part of the house I saw faint tattered souls and then bigger things milling about and they weren't good, then one turned and looked at me. I opened my eyes and stood up and I felt dizzy so I went back into the other room. The others turned and asked me "what's wrong." I stood there and these scratches welted up and appeared on my forehead as they watched, and they were filmed.

Adam later explained to me the meaning of the scratches: "The typical demonic scratch is in threes like cat scratches. It will follow the lines of the body with no skips. Demons love to do things in threes. They want to terrify you by marking you so you know you can be physically harmed. The goal is to wear you down to the point where you submit to possession."

That night as I slept I had a very disturbing dream in which all of the money issues and related emotions, especially the anger, I had toward Lesa came flooding back into my head. I knew that it was being done to distract me, but it was very difficult to manage for some time after I was awake. The dream also included a detailed scene in which she went to court because of unpaid bills and Kerry represented her. This thing certainly was going all out to attack my mind.

Father Mike arrived around noon, and for most of the afternoon five of us, Fr. Mike, me, Kerry, Ryan, and Adam, sat in the living room and discussed what had taken place in the house, recently and over the long term. The rest of Ryan's team was positioned around the house and monitored their equipment.

I spoke with Fr. Ron on the phone late in the afternoon and told him what had happened with the team.

"I can feel the tension coming from the house like a nuclear reactor ready to melt down," he told me, with an unfamiliar worried tone in his voice. "They should not have called upon the demon to tell them its name or to reveal itself to them. That was very dangerous. Please, all of you need to be very careful tonight."

We had dinner, and afterward Fr. Mike began a prayer session that lasted about two hours. Lesa, Kerry, Adam, and I participated as Ryan attended to the rest of his team. Father Mike wanted to interject spiritual power into the house while the demon was apparently active, angry, and possibly vulnerable. I knew that he was not happy that everyone in the house didn't attend. I disagreed. This team was not here to pray but to observe and document. Despite this the prayers were very direct and powerful. Fr. Ron was also concerned about a team member "who wore a leather jacket." There in fact was one young man who had a leather jacket, and I was advised to watch him, as he might become violent. He also told me to put away a pair of scissors that were lying out on a table. They were, and I did.

At 8:00 P.M. we officially began the cleansing ceremony preceded by the rite designed for a dwelling. We then began on the third floor with prayer, candles, incense, holy water, and a crucifix. Fr. Mike started with a prayer:

Loving God we praise and thank you for your mercy and love, your healing power, your deliverance, and freedom from the evil. We take the authority you have given us over the power of darkness and rebuke Satan in Jesus' name and Beelzebub and all the demons and all the forces of evil that seek to control and attack this house and property and the Cranmer Family.

We thank you for the little ones, we pray this may be a place of safety for them as well. We come against the smells, the foul smell of Satan, may the sweet smell of incense overcome them. May the movie *The Passion of the Christ* cleanse this room and all the house and drive away whatever evil has been there. Watch over each person in their coming and going. We come against the evil and sinfulness that occurred in this house especially the women and children harmed and the loss of life at the hands of an evil man. We reject him in the name of Jesus, may no remnant be here in any form. We come against that furnace that may have been the place these remains were burned. We pray that may be cleansed.

Bless be the name of the Lord. May the joy of the Lord be the Cranmer family's strength. May they continue to celebrate the name of the Lord in this house that belongs to them and was given to them.

While we were working our way through the third floor, Ryan was on the second floor in the blue room where the *The Passion* was playing. He said that all of a sudden a sexless apparition came out of the closet and smiled at him in a mocking manner and then disappeared back into the closet. This was nothing new for my family, but it startled Ryan badly. We continued through the rest of the house down to the basement and did not let this event distract us. The entire house was cleansed, and when the ceremony was concluded we gathered again in the living room.

During the cleansing my son David related what occurred in his and Charlie's room, as I was downstairs with Fr. Mike.

The lights were off and the moonlight was coming in the bedroom and Charlie, Kerry, and I were all standing there praying. Some of the PRS people were there, too. When we got to the fireplace by the closet door even though there was light coming in from the windows that one corner became overwhelmed by darkness, you couldn't see the fireplace at all, nothing. It was like a black cloud suddenly appeared in front of the open closet. We held hands and prayed and boxed it into the corner. Charlie and I both yelled:

"Get out of our room" and the darkness went back into the corner.

Then we yelled, "In the name of Jesus get out of our room."

Only at that point could we see our fireplace. The smell was really bad, too!

Adam later explained that when a demon is not pretending to be in a grotesque human form it will appear as a black smoke. "You can't see through it, but it will dissipate as it leaves. The smallest form is the size of a large egg, as if mice were running along the floor, except it glides up the walls and ceilings, in the shape of small black blobs. Some people will see different sizes, depending on the potency of the spirits. People often say they see a black cat or black dog out of the corner of their eye even though they have no pets. In that black smoke form the spirit can tumble and move but doesn't leave anything behind it. We have some photos of that captured with cell phone cameras. When they're pretending to be human," he went on, "you'll see a four foot tall humanoid-looking form, which moves like a person but is also completely black with no features. The higher ranked one is man-sized, a very solid silhouette."

This is what was seen in our home many times over the years.

I learned about the other characteristics of demons from Adam. In some instances they may pretend to be the ghost of someone you know, like your deceased grandmother. This is how they con people into interacting. But the hallmark of demons pretending to be something else is there's always something deformed or missing. The head will be down so they're hiding their eyes, the face is deformed, the legs are animal legs, or the legs are missing and they're pulling themselves along the floor. There's always something wrong. Most commonly they don't make a physical appearance you can see at all. Most times they just create havoc, attack people, and cause problems without being visible.

We all reconvened later in the living room about 11:00 P.M. and closed with a prayer. It had been a long day and I was particularly exhausted. I once again felt a sense of satisfaction that we had met the demon on its own terms. A toll was taken on both sides, and the war wasn't over, but a major confrontation had just occurred and everyone had done their part. Fr. Mike and Kerry left the house and we went to bed while various members of the PRS team stayed awake with their equipment throughout the night.

I was up early, and at about 9:00 A.M. my friend Tom Murphy, still the mayor of Pittsburgh at the time, stopped by to meet some of the team from Penn State.

We sat around the dining room table talking about how evil entities play a role in all kinds of heinous crimes and gang violence without anyone being aware of it.

"Evil is not just in this house, you know," I said. "It's dominated this entire community for years. Isn't it strange that this little community had the first drive-by shooting in Pittsburgh, and mob-connected nightclubs not long ago, and is known as a deeply racist town?"

Connie later said the effect of the demon in my house was like the ripples from a drop of water. "The evil in your house rippled out all over the town," was the way she put it.

The mayor talked about all of the senseless violence committed by young men, generally against one another, and what role evil might play in initiating and driving it. We went on to have a general roundtable discussion about how evil dominates and influences the world, lurking subtly and silently behind the headlines and news reports that one hears daily concerning unbridled violence, either locally or on the world stage.

Adam wondered about mass shootings. "How does a teenage kid from a normal middle-class family all of a sudden shoot up his entire school one day? I think these killers are influenced and directly driven by the demonic. No one thinks that the Devil is real, that evil is an actual entity able to turn vulnerable people into killers. These days people assume that evil, apart from human emotions, is just some medieval superstition."

I thought about the hollow eyes and blank stares that you see on the face of these killers, like the girls who did the bidding of Charles Manson. They looked and acted as though they were puppets working from someone else's evil direction.

We also discussed Hitler and the Holocaust, a prime example of evil emerging inexplicably from an advanced industrial, scientific, and educated nation. I have always felt that the Nazi killing machine is incomprehensible without it being the direct work of the demonic. These Nazis got up in the morning, had breakfast, kissed their wives good-bye, petted their dogs, and went out and tortured and killed millions of people, including children. How else do you explain that?

Kerry, who is very knowledgeable and likes to share his erudition, added, "The Devil isn't brought up much in churches anymore because people simply don't believe in it," he said. "That's convenient because the demonic wants to remain hidden and anonymous. In fact there's a quote from the famous poet Charles Baudelaire that 'the greatest trick the Devil ever pulled is to convince us all that he does not exist.'"

Listening quietly to this conversation I knew that it all made sense. For years we thought that we were living with Casper the Friendly Ghost. Now that it was exposed, it had dropped this pretense and was showing us fully what was behind the mask. I felt reassured that my family now knew the truth about evil's presence in the world. Forewarned is forearmed, as they say.

The PRS team stayed that afternoon and then packed up and left that evening. Their visit had once again been eventful and had accomplished the purpose I had hoped for. This was an interesting group of bright young people, and they had done an admirable, if not heroic, job. In hindsight their two visits were somewhat messy affairs, like lancing the outer surface of an infected wound, especially in opening up the area under the staircase. Hopefully we could now treat the infection with our holy antibiotics.

CHAPTER TWENTY-TWO

Even after the visit from PRS and the discovery of the demon's lair, in February 2005 the conclusion of this battle was still not in sight. In fact the demon seemed to be energized and stronger than ever.

Fr. Mike was still suspicious of PRS. Even though he agreed that the deliverance session that we had while they were there was extremely effective, he was wary of the highly publicized case file about us now on the Internet. In fact within weeks of their second visit to the house there were pictures and a video posted for viewing on their website. Ryan had agreed to keep our family name and the actual location of the house confidential, but he did refer to it as the "Pittsburgh Hell-mouth." I thought that this was a little over the top, but this was in fact a big case for PRS. Ryan would later write about it as "one of the most influential and dangerous cases he was involved with, and it changed the course of PRS forever." I sent an e-mail to Ryan to reemphasize our agreement of anonymity, and he reaffirmed that agreement. I told him that this was not the time for publicity; in fact it was the last thing that we needed. The website was filled with a lot of hype, and Ryan apparently had quite a following, but I couldn't begrudge them; this was what they did. And to their credit, when I contacted them they were at our door just like ghost-busters, no pun intended.

But I also realized that Fr. Mike was correct, and Julie had even confided to him that several members of the PRS team were psychologically traumatized by their visits to the house. She feared for the team's safety if they continued to be involved. From my standpoint, they had fulfilled their original purpose of verification and documentation, and continued involvement would not be constructive or useful. From the perspective of actually forcing this thing to leave, they had no more to contribute; that challenge would still be up to us. First and foremost I had to keep the priests working together. PRS agreed to provide a report of their activities to the diocese, which was fine for the purpose of outside verification, but I didn't particularly need a report; I was there with them. I admired the PRS team and appreciated their efforts, but now it was time to get on with the day-to-day battle of fighting to expel this thing from our home.

The demon's activity had not diminished; in fact it had increased. The blood spattering had now moved down to the first floor and appeared on the entire length of the two staircases, in the library, and also on the kitchen cabinets. When I removed the wallpaper in the first-floor library it was on the plaster walls under the paper as well.

Fr. Mike had advised me to remove the door knocker from the door of the blue room. Fr. Ron had told us that it was used to control access while the doctor was doing his ghastly business but had not told me to remove it. Some contention arose between them about who was in charge of this issue, but I just ignored it. The next morning I threw it into the Monongahela River from the 10th Street Bridge as I drove to work. Fr. Mike thought that since it had been directly associated with the evil deeds that its removal might have some further impact upon the demon. That evening as Charlie went into the small bedroom to practice guitar he discovered that the crucifix had been thrown off of the wall and was lying facedown in the middle of the floor. Where the crucifix had hung there were drops of the spattered blood running down the wall. As he sat there and played, he heard what sounded like nails being scratched across a blackboard.

That night as I was lying in bed I was scratched on the leg so hard it woke me up. It felt as if I had been jabbed and scraped with a needle or sharp pin. This thing was moving around the house at will, displaying what seemed to be a temper tantrum. I could almost feel its frustration, which again convinced me that we had to push back and persevere.

Fr. Ron gave me a formal prayer to add to my daily ritual to be spoken each morning before I left the house. It read as follows:

In the name of Jesus, this is my house and my family. I call the angels of the Lord for protection and ask that a golden light be placed around my house and property. I ask Jesus that the demons be made silent and forced to remain restrained in quiet sleep so that we can live in this house in peace and harmony as a family. In the name of Jesus I pray that this evil ultimately be expelled. Amen.

These weren't exactly the words I would have chosen, but Fr. Ron had been on the mark so far, and I certainly wasn't one to question directives from headquarters; my job was to carry them out, and that's what I did.

We planned for a discussion meeting and prayer session for the first Saturday in March to assess where we were at with the current situation in the house. Attending with Lesa and me would be Fr. Mike, Kerry, and Barb, the psychic who worked with Fr. Mike. In the days prior to this session the demon began to attack Lesa and me with some very bizarre dreams, the type that are so real it takes several minutes after being startled awake to realize it's not actually happening. Lesa told me that she had one dream twice and it was so real, she was convinced it affected her physically.

"There was a large triangle in a square downstairs in the house surrounded by black-cloaked figures with candles chanting, 'Moloch.' It was terrifying, like a witches' coven. In the center was an extremely large being draped in black moving back and forth with a large sword. All of a sudden the being plunges the sword into one of the other figures.

That's when I woke up. This morning my knee felt as if it were on fire." She was trembling as she told me this.

I looked at her knee and there was in fact a small puncture wound.

The following night I dreamed that Lesa had died, and I went through the entire funeral process and procession before I was startled awake. I didn't get upset, however, because I was aware of what the spirit was trying to do. It wasn't working and we weren't afraid of it. In fact I joked to Lesa, "Well, except for the blood running down the walls everything is pretty normal in our house, don't you think?"

Below is the text of two e-mails that we sent to each other the next day that express how we felt at the time.

Sent: Thursday, March 03, 2005 2:29 PM
To: Cranmer, Lesa A
Subject: I finally see the pattern

Lesa:

This thing tries to destroys us mentally, tries to turn us against each other, hurts us physically, moves us to hurt ourselves, and hurt each other, runs me out of the house, attempts to ruin us financially, tries to break up our marriage, starts moving pictures and furniture, stinks up the rooms to scare us, puts blood on the walls to intimidate us, now it is trying to scare us psychologically through our dreams, what's next in its bag of tricks? We must continue to pray and love each other until it gives up.

- - - - - - - - - - - - - -

To: Bob
From: "Cranmer, Lesa A" 3/3/2005 2:39 PM

Bob,

Charlie said that he could not sleep last night. The smell
was down in the basement really strong when I went
down to do the laundry. No matter what happens we all
have to keep an even temper and not let things get to
us. We have to make sure that we are praising the boys.
Bobby told me last night that he loves me! You could
have knocked me over with a feather!

Lesa

The next day the discussion and prayer meeting took
place, and we prayed again room by room throughout the
entire house. We discussed all of the positive developments within our family, especially with Bobby, who had
found a very nice new girlfriend who was a good influence on him. He had met her years before at church camp.

But despite these positive developments, the night
after the prayer meeting Lesa was pushed down and her
feet were knocked out from under her at the foot of the
main staircase as she was coming up to bed. Her shoulder
hit a statue and it fell and broke into pieces. I was already
upstairs in the bathroom getting ready for bed, and it
sounded as if a fight had broken out in the foyer. I rushed
down to help her and saw what had happened.

"Did it knock you down?" I asked.

"Yes, once again," she responded, sighing and sounding resigned, like it was no big deal.

I was furious. "If I could see it I'd like to have a crack at it sometime!" I told her.

After this happened I had a restless night and awoke about 5:00 A.M. extremely anxious that the thing was creeping around the house. I prayed the rosary and lay back down.

The following day, the doorknob to David's room turned back and forth while he was in the room playing his video game after school. The door was then locked from the outside as it had been with Charlie once before. This thing was not letting up, but I did sense desperation in its actions. It seemed to be doing anything and everything now to unsettle us, and it wasn't working. We'd even gotten used to the blood on the walls. Something was happening in the spiritual realm; I just wasn't certain what it meant. What could we expect next from this thing?

For the next several weeks, things were peaceful in the house, almost normal. It was a wonderful respite considering all we had been through during January and February. Bobby and Charlie finally seemed to have come through the worst and were doing well. Bobby got his driver's license, and Charlie was temporarily in a private school equipped to deal with his fragile emotional condition. He was slowly recovering and had altogether stopped the self-destructive behavior that had been such a concern.

David, who had never really been affected by the situation, now showed a new level of independence and maturity. From this point forward he seemed to go his own way and do his own thing apart from his two brothers. He had participated in many of the deliverance sessions and boldly announced one day that he was moving into the blue room and moved his bed and clothes in before I knew it. I could not take issue with his boldness or his bravery. He was going to take the room back single-handedly! I suppose he came by those traits naturally. The next month he would join the Marines on the deferred entry program. Not long after he graduated high school in June, he left for boot camp at Parris Island, South Carolina.

Bobby had moved into the master bedroom where I had battled the demon and its stench for months but there was now only an occasional trace of it. We were taking ground back from the demon, and it felt good for a change. I kept the movie playing for a few more weeks in the small maid's room that Bobby had vacated.

The Passion of the Christ played on the second floor of our house for seven months straight, twenty-four hours a day. I would watch it when saying my nightly prayers, and I faithfully knew every scene, every word, and every movement. The Devil is known to be repelled by scenes of the Passion and the crucifixion, and there was even a portrayal of Christ's triumph over Satan in the film. Controversial as the film may have been, along with its creator, for me it was simply a continuous artillery barrage against the forces of the Evil One. I will testify to its power, for I witnessed and experienced it firsthand, and it gave me strength as well.

I had moved my dressing room and a small office onto the third floor right before the blood had first appeared in January. I would soon discover that it would follow me there and this would be an active battleground. One night I was going through a box of things from my deceased mother's house and I came across a card I had received from the Vatican in 1963. I was a Cub Scout then and my mother was our den mother. She had each of us in our den write a letter to Pope John thanking him for all he was doing at the time, and we had each received a personal reply. With this card was a picture of me in my Cub Scout uniform that I had not seen in years.

Later that night I was looking for something in the trash basket and to my surprise I found the picture there. Believing that I had somehow inadvertently thrown it away, I thought nothing of it. But to my surprise that night when I was getting ready for bed I saw the picture in the small trash can in the bathroom. Fr. Ron later told me that there was much spiritual energy surrounding this picture because of its association with the memory and the love of my mother, as well as the Vatican project she had us do. These odd developments never ceased to amaze me.

Two different types of stench soon began to emerge in these rooms on the third floor. In the outer hallway and steps there would be a sweet smell of fresh blood. Inside the rooms there would be a very pronounced odor of something rotten. Almost like a sickeningly strong body odor. It would appear for a few minutes and then disappear. It was at this time I began to have somewhat routine one-sided conversations with the demon that I always started with "In the name of Jesus." I would tell it that I wasn't impressed and that it could stink the place up all it wanted, we were not going to relent, we were not leaving, but that it soon would be. Sometimes I would laugh when talking to it.

On the twenty-third of March I came home and went

to the third floor to change. I made a habit of keeping this area locked since I knew that the activity was now centered there. When I went into the room I was quite surprised to find a small stripe of blood on the back of one of my white cotton dress shirts that was hanging on a clothes tree. I didn't get alarmed and simply tossed the shirt aside. I loudly made another strongly worded comment about the demon's eventual departure and reiterated that I wasn't at all impressed.

On Easter Sunday Bobby drove us all to Mass. Fr. Mike stopped by the house and had a private conversation with Charlie that went very well. I was beginning to understand that each of us had to defeat this thing in our own manner. It was losing its grip on us as well as on the house. The evil was truly being overcome with our love for one another, as all of its machinations were failing to cause the intended results.

During the first week in April the activity began to pick up on the first floor with the puddles of clear and red substances appearing once again. While taking pictures of some new blood on the walls, I was coming down the steps and saw our dog at the foot of the staircase staring up at me motionless in one of his hypnotic trances (I called it his terminal stare). I quickly held the camera up and took a picture of him from the landing halfway up. A few days later Lesa picked up the developed pictures. She called me and said, "You're not going to believe this." We were astonished to see what appeared to be a smoky skeleton-like figure directly in front of me in the picture. I had always suspected the dog was looking directly at the spirit.

The evil spirit began what appeared to be another temper tantrum and started moving things around on the first floor. Early on Saturday morning as I was leaving the house for Mass at the convent, I discovered the cabinets in the kitchen open and containers and other items scattered all over the floor. The extra grocery bags that Lesa kept were strewn over the basement steps. When Lesa turned the basement lights on, both bulbs controlled by the switch burned out at the same time. The glass top to a decorative kerosene lamp was placed inside the music compartment of our old pump organ while Lesa's car keys were found on top of the grandfather clock in the foyer.

But these were all childish pranks that seemed to be more of a nuisance than a threat. If this was all that it could muster up, I thought that our continuous pressure was finally breaking its will. But this turned out to be merely another lull. We had more challenges to face. However intermittent the strikes at us had become, the battle wasn't over quite yet. There was still activity in the closet with the pull chain on the light. One afternoon when Lesa had the door to the closet open, the cat casually walked into the closet and proceeded into the area under the steps. Within a few seconds Lesa said that the cat shot out of the space like a rocket and hid somewhere in the house.

With this incident, I had an idea and decided to conduct an experiment. This thing could take on some type of physical form that could be seen at times, so there must be some type of physical consistency to it. I knew that it had properties beyond scientific understanding, but I thought that I'd try a simple test. I knew that it spent time in the closet area under the steps. Even though we had opened it up, it was still empty. I took about ten feet of exposed copper wire and strung two strands of it inside the space under the steps, effectively dividing it in half. I left about an inch between the two wires to ensure the two did not come close to touching. I then closed off the space with a large piece of wood. From the basement below I had run an electric cord and had carefully attached the positive and negative current to the two wires in the space. With the area effectively sealed off I told Lesa that the closet itself was "off-limits" for a few days. I plugged the cord into live current and waited. As long as nothing disturbed the wires and contact between them was not made there would be no problem. If contact was made a switch in the breaker box would immediately be tripped and I would know that I had possibly gotten the thing's attention. (For those electricians who are reading, I did take all of the proper precautions to insulate the wires, and the only place where they were exposed was in the air.) I left it in place for about a week with no results, so either the thing knew what I was trying to do, or it was impervious to electricity.

But the mere act of my laying a trap for it made a statement about where this battle stood. I was the aggressor and it was being stalked. As far as the space went, Lesa came up with the best idea for how to deal with it. One weekend she had the boys bring all of the Christmas decorations down from the attic room and literally filled the space with boxes. We claimed the area with the items that brought us happiness and joy. This ended up being a much better maneuver than the electric wires, and probably packed a stronger punch than 110 volts.

The simple act of filling the demon's lair with Christmas decorations had the desired impact. I believe this meant it was unable to retreat and recharge for further assaults. Slowly our house began to take on a state of normalcy and a peace settled in over the family. There were still some struggles with Charlie at times, but we dealt with them effectively. Lesa and I had arranged for all of us (including Jessica, Tom, and the grandchildren—Jessica now had two sons) to spend a week on the island of Nantucket. We rented a large house in June and looked upon it as a time for the family to get some R and R from the battlefield. David would be leaving for the Marines at the end of the month, and it would be the last time we would all be together as a family for a while.

CHAPTER TWENTY-THREE

Fr. Ron had always maintained that by doing our best to live life as normally as possible we would be helping ourselves and the situation as well. I was able to maintain an efficient level of performance at work because I viewed it as a relief. But the situation in the house had taken a toll on me—a more substantial toll than I realized.

Something besides the battle in the house had been weighing heavily on me for years—my unfinished political business—addressing the long-standing issues with the police department in Brentwood. It was another fight that I wanted to finish. I had been waiting for five years to run for mayor, and the election was approaching. Unfortunately the timing wasn't opportune. I was still engaged with the battle in the house and still distracted by the issues with my sons, although they were diminishing. Nonetheless, I just couldn't pass up the opportunity. Brentwood is a small community, and it was a small municipal election, with less than two thousand votes being cast. Compared to the several hundred thousand votes of my previous county election, I thought it would be a walk in the park. It only took ten signatures to get my name on the ballot in March, and there would be no primary challenge. I could easily do some direct mail in the fall, and that would be the extent of it. I was anxious to take on the evil in the community as well as what remained in the house. Kerry didn't think it was a good idea when I asked him.

"Bob, you're not superhuman. You're dealing daily with an adversary who can be counted on to be unpredictable. Your family is very fragile emotionally. They need you now."

"I won't get another crack at this for four years," I responded. "Who knows what will take place by then. Now is the time to do it. I have to clean the place up once and for all!"

"Why do you have to run at all, Bob?" he asked. "I thought you were through with politics."

"It's time I finished the job I started when I was on council, getting rid of the corruption in this town. I'm cleaning up the house. I'll take care of Brentwood as well."

Kerry continued to insist this was an absolutely foolhardy decision, considering all that I was involved with in my own home, and he ended up being correct. I had no idea that there were forces at work in the town who knew very well the corruption I planned to clean up if I were elected. They also knew that their livelihoods could be at stake if I were mayor and I shut down the illegal gambling interests. In a surprise move, a candidate appeared as an "independent" from nowhere in August—the proprietor of one of the local taverns. I soon discovered that I had very little focus or time to campaign, whereas the forces against me campaigned like their very lives depended upon it. I tried but never had a chance despite spending thousands of dollars on direct mail pieces. I wondered if they were all even delivered. Running as a Republican anywhere in 2005 was difficult, but even more so when the registration was over two to one against you.

I came in third in the three-way race, and it was a huge embarrassment. I had never lost an election and this was a bitter pill, but Kerry had been correct all along. It wasn't the right time or the right thing to do. I had taken on way too much because I believed I was invincible. I thought that if I was determined to become mayor of Brentwood I would succeed—that I could do anything, as the Lord was always with me. We all make mistakes, and this had been the mistake of all mistakes for me. A few years earlier I had been considered a viable Republican candidate for lieutenant governor but had now lost an insignificant municipal election. It was the definitive end of my political career. I had completely underestimated the animosity the town still had for me. Nonetheless, I still had another battle to fight and win.

The months of April and May passed with no major activity other than some small harassment and items disappearing and mysteriously reappearing. I received a report from the lab that analyzed the bloodlike substance on the walls. The report concluded that it was not real blood. The mysterious substance contained mildew, spores, and some skin cells, but it was also not any type of mold or natural growth. To me it made little difference if it was real or not. I was more concerned with how it got there.

On June 1, 2005, both Fr. Mike and Fr. Ed came by to celebrate Mass in the living room. Strangely enough both our dog and cat sat in the room throughout the Mass with us. I knew that they were both aware of this evil spirit and were in a way as involved with the struggle as we were. The cat seemed to be very sensitive and now regularly slept at night in the doorway to our bedroom; our dog was now so old that he couldn't negotiate steps and had to be carried.

Later in the week a completely unexpected development occurred that took me by surprise. Jessica called me one Saturday afternoon from her house—the small duplex I rented for them—and asked me to come right over. It was only a few blocks away. When I entered the house she took me directly to the stairs.

"Look at this," she said. On the white wall of the staircase were very fine streaks of the bloodlike substance.

I cleaned it off and placed the towel in a plastic bag that I later burned.

"I also saw a black shape out of the corner of my eye the previous day, Dad," she said, looking at me with an uncharacteristically panicked expression. I was upset by this since Jessica was usually unflappable.

"I'm so sorry this is happening," I said, in what I hoped was a reassuring tone of voice. I put my arm around her and gave her a hug. "I really thought that moving you and Collin would keep you safe. Let's hope this is just a reverberation of what's happened at our house and not a major infestation." In fact, I had to admit to myself that I was very worried as well.

This manifestation at Jessica's may have explained why things had been so quiet in our house for the past month. This evil was unbelievable in the lengths it was willing to go just to get to me, since it knew that my grandchildren were my weak spot. It was showing me that the measures I had taken to protect them were not enough to keep them out of its grasp. There wasn't much I could do about it at this point, however, other than pray in her house and report the incident to Fr. Ron. We would soon be leaving for our family vacation, and I would deal with it when we returned.

Our trip to the island of Nantucket was a wonderful experience. We stayed in Hyannis Port for a night and then caught the ferry to Nantucket for the two-hour trip. We spent the week exploring the island, riding bikes, and eating out. I didn't forget what awaited us at home when we returned, so I went to Mass every morning while there, at a little parish named St. Mary's in the town. David left for boot camp when we returned.

When we got back the problems were still present in Jessica's house. In fact, they got worse. Both she and Collin had their legs swept out from under them while coming down the steps. I arranged to pick up Fr. Ed one afternoon to go to her house to celebrate Mass. We had a peaceful time and he also went through and blessed each room. From that day on, Jessica and her family didn't experience any other problems in the house.

The next day however, the activity began again in the main house, which for me was a relief. The entity had been driven back or possibly had to return. It would be hard to say what rules govern the activity of these beings. Maybe they can't concentrate on more than one place at a time.

Since David had moved into the blue room, I had moved my daily morning and nightly prayers into the small bedroom where my aunt had died. I would pray in the morning before leaving for work and then again at night I would pray the rosary before bed. I had the two prayers that Fr. Ron had given me printed on pieces of white paper that I recited from. One night in late July as I was praying, my heavy black rosary fell apart right in my hands. As I examined the pieces, I could see that the metal links were still closed and intact; in fact I had to bend them open with pliers to put it back together again. The next night as I went into the room to pray I could not find Fr. Ron's printed prayers anywhere. I looked through the entire room and then checked the other bedrooms as well. I went back into the small room to start again and just noticed the corner of a piece of folded paper sticking out about a half inch from behind a picture on the wall. I pulled the picture out, and one of the prayers fell to the floor from behind it. As I got down on my knee to pick it up, I noticed the other prayer had been slipped down in a crack between the ten-inch baseboard and the wall. It was obvious that these two pieces of paper were purposely hidden from me. This told me one thing: that my praying was having an impact. I drew strength and confidence from this incident.

I then began to experience "knocking" on the walls when I was praying, and early one Saturday morning, as I was getting ready to go to the convent 7:15 Mass, there was a very loud knock on the front door. I was in the library right next to the door so I quickly opened the door and of course there was no one there, but then I didn't expect there would be.

Despite these incidents, things had settled down quite a bit from where we had been months earlier. But the spirit was still present in the house. I knew that we had to take the battle to a higher level once again. I didn't want to bring the Penn State group back, because Fr. Mike had serious issues with them now and they had played no effective role in actually cleansing the house. Something or someone more powerful was needed at this point. The thing seemed to be in a seriously weakened state, but it needed to be made vulnerable enough to hit with that one final knockout blow. I spoke with Fr. Mike about it and he agreed.

CHAPTER TWENTY-FOUR

A few months earlier Fr. Ron had mentioned that he was considering accessing the expertise and experience of the chief exorcist of the Archdiocese of New York, Fr. James LeBar. In fact, that's the primary reason he wanted the outside verification of the activity. He felt even then that the situation in the house had risen to such a level that calling in a Church expert was warranted. PRS had verified the haunting so the Church could move forward with a trained exorcist. He had already initiated the process.

I looked up Fr. LeBar and found that he was famous. In 1991 he conducted an exorcism in Palm Beach, Florida, which was broadcast on the ABC TV program *20/20*. He was appointed the chief exorcist of the New York Archdiocese in 1992, by Cardinal John Joseph O'Connor. An expert on Satanism and cults, he's been interviewed on a number of TV shows, including the Geraldo Rivera television program exploring satanic ritual abuse in 1995. He was also a consultant to the movie *Lost Souls* in 1999.

Fr. Ron had contacted Fr. LeBar, and he was willing to come to Pittsburgh if the need was verified and a formal request was made. It would now be determined by Bishop Wuerl if the request would be made from the Pittsburgh Diocese to the Archdiocese of New York. At that time Fr. Ron had asked me to provide him with a synopsis of the whole story to be used as documentation in making the request. I wasn't sure what this priest was going to do that hadn't already been done, but then Fr. LeBar's visit was put off due to a medical condition, as he was elderly and in fragile health. After he delayed the trip, the diocese had also decided to wait. However, I thought the time for waiting was over and the opportunity to end this situation once and for all was upon us. We needed to get another exorcist.

Fr. Ron thought it wasn't a good idea. He felt that if things were slowly settling down and the house was quiet, why should we attempt to stir things up again? For the first time I firmly disagreed with him. Yes, it was quiet, but was the thing gone from our lives and our home? No. I had recently placed a picture of the new pope on the wall where the blood had first appeared on the third floor. It was there for several days until I found it lying facedown outside the room on the steps. This thing was still as malevolent as ever, and we could not peacefully coexist with it even in a weakened form. It had to be expelled. We had to press the issue.

Once Fr. LeBar was contacted, everything went into motion. His health improved, and the required approvals were finally coordinated. A date in September 2005 was set for his visit to the house, and Fr. LeBar was provided with the synopsis document I had prepared several months earlier.

Big news travels fast, and in the demonic world I suppose even faster. It wasn't long before the stench began to appear throughout the house again, and on one particular Friday night in mid-August it was very strong at the top of the steps. I had just finished my prayers around midnight and was headed for bed. As I stood underneath a large five-paddle ceiling fan that hangs over the space looking down into the foyer, the smell was thick in the air. Later that night I woke up in a cold sweat and found that I was completely turned around in bed and that my head was at the bottom of the bed and my feet were on the pillow. I found it very difficult to move and was in a daze, to the point that when the alarm went off at 6:00 A.M. I was unable to turn it off or get out of bed to go to Mass as I always did on Saturday mornings.

Lesa and I both began to have very strange, perverted dreams that I can't even write about because they were so bizarre. Then the following night as Lesa got up to go into the bathroom I heard a loud crash and jumped out of bed to find her lying on the floor. She had been pushed so hard against the corner of the wall that the force had actually broken the skin. As I helped her up, she said that she had been shoved in the darkness. This thing was attacking us again. It had to stop.

The day finally came for Fr. LeBar's visit. He arrived at the airport that afternoon and was going to stay overnight at the monastery. He was met by a young Byzantine Catholic priest named Fr. Ben who came with him to the house. The two of them together looked as if they came from central casting for *The Exorcist* movie. Fr. LeBar was the older priest, with a very serious demeanor, somewhat frail looking, while Fr. Ben resembled a young, handsome movie star with dark black hair and a square jaw. I was very encouraged. I felt as if the John Wayne of the antidemonic world had come to the house and there was going to be a final shoot-out at last with this thing.

In addition to these two priests, in attendance were Fr. Mike, Fr. Ed, Kerry, Barb, Lesa, and myself. Everyone arrived at the house at 6:30 P.M., and after brief introductions we went right to work in the living room. I spent about an hour or so discussing the history of the infestation and all of the activity. Fr. Mike and Kerry added to this, and there was in-depth analysis as to the degree of this infestation by Fr. LeBar. I concluded from his comments that he categorized our case as a strong and somewhat unique demonic infestation. Fr. Mike and I both commented that the situation seemed to have been broken wide open during the two visits by the group from Penn State. The activity, now somewhat sporadic, had continued with varying degrees of intensity. Psychological attacks had persisted, but all in all the family seemed much better prepared to deal with them now than we had been initially.

After this discussion Fr. Mike and Fr. LeBar consulted as to the roles of all present and then initiated a Catholic prayer ritual designed to defeat the demon, bind it, and cast it out of the house. It started:

O Most illustrious prince of the heavenly hosts, holy Michael the Archangel, from thy heavenly throne defend us in the battle against the princes and powers, against the rulers of the world's darkness. Come to the assistance of humankind, whom God has created in His own image and likeness, and whom He has purchased at a great price from Satan's tyranny. Thee the holy Church does venerate as her patron and guardian. To thee the Lord has entrusted the service of leading the souls of the redeemed into heavenly blessedness. Intercede for us to the God of peace, that He would crush Satan under our feet, lest he any longer have power to hold men captive and do harm to the Church. Present our prayers at the throne of the Most High, so that He may all the more speedily favor us with His mercy. Lay hold of the dragon, the ancient serpent, no other than the demon, Satan, and cast him bound into the abyss, so that he may no longer seduce mankind.

In the name of Jesus Christ, our Lord and God, with confidence in the intercession of the Virgin Mary, Mother of God, of blessed Michael the Archangel, of the holy apostles Peter and Paul, and all the saints, and with assurance in the sacred power of our ministry, we steadfastly proceed with the task of expelling the molestations of the Devil's frauds.

I was anticipating that something profound was going to occur but all was normal. No thunder, no crashes, no levitation, but I did not sense the presence of the demon.

I knew it well and could smell it and feel when it was around—and it wasn't there. I imagined two large angels dragging its pitiful presence down the steps in chains. All was peaceful in the room as we prayed. Something of significance was happening.

This ceremony lasted only about a half hour, and Fr. LeBar remained seated in the living room, presiding over the house with his spiritual and holy aura, while the rest of us began the standard cleansing process with the prayer to St. Michael:

St. Michael the Archangel, defend us in battle; be our protection against the wickedness and snares of the Devil. May God rebuke him, we humbly pray.

And do thou, O prince of the heavenly host, by the power of God cast into Hell Satan and all of the evil spirits who prowl about the world seeking the ruin of souls. Amen.

I had been through this drill so many times it had become routine, but this time things seemed to be different. There was an air of authority, like we were walking through a combat zone that was now empty and littered with the remains of the struggle.

Lesa and I each carried a candle from our home altar as we started on the third floor. When we entered the attic room Fr. Ben said that he sensed a "void" and asked if anything of significance had ever occurred there. I responded that this was the room where the spirit had appeared over Collin's bed and I had fought it there with scripture for four nights and it had scratched my neck pretty seriously.

Each area in the house represented a different phase of the struggle. Almost every room was significant; two had at one point been lost to the demon, then subsequently we had taken them back.

While in the basement, we spent extra time in the furnace room because it disturbed Barb. She said that she sensed evil in the room. Fr. Ed and Kerry had remained on the second floor to pray, and the group then went outside. The front yard was blessed, and Fr. Mike spent time blessing the infamous rosebush in the backyard as well. At this point, we went back into the house and everyone reassembled in the living room where Fr. LeBar had remained.

Barb told us that she had a vision of a demon in chains looking up from beneath us and asked that we go back down to the furnace room, which is directly under the living room. While there, she began to sweat and commented on how extremely hot it was in the room. It wasn't unusually hot in the room, as the furnace was not operating, but you could tell that she was hot because her face was beet red. Fr. Mike and Fr. Ben prayed and blessed the room once again. We all went back to the living room where Fr. Ed prayed the rosary. By this time, it was approaching 9:30 P.M. and we concluded in prayer.

Fr. LeBar said that we should expect "echo" events to occasionally occur for some months into the future but not to be alarmed; this for some reason was natural and would eventually stop. Everyone said their thanks and good-byes and left around 10:00 P.M.

I felt good about what had taken place but still uneasy that there was no event that signified closure, and was unsettled with Barb's experience in the furnace room. I sensed that the entire battlefield was not ours, but only time would tell.

A few days later the younger priest, Fr. Ben, sent me a message that gave us great encouragement. He thanked us for our hospitality and relayed his hope that all was well in our home. He mentioned that as Fr. LeBar had stated, there could be one last bit of demonic retribution, but he hoped there wouldn't be. He referenced personal friends of his who'd been through a similar ordeal and again reiterated his sorrow over how long we had to live with the demonic infestation. Fr. Ben said that God was glorified because we had taken on the battle and expressed his best wishes for myself and my family. He offered to continue to pray for us and asked that we do the same for him.

(As it turned out, Fr. Ron had known Fr. Ben when he was a young boy—he was a parish priest in Fr. Ben's town of Butler, Pennsylvania—and I thought it interesting that they would come together years later on the case. Fr. Ron, reticent about his past, never mentioned the connection at the time.)

A powerful cast had been assembled in the house that evening, and it was the strong assault on the demon I had been looking for, but unfortunately, as I suspected, it wouldn't prove to be the definitive ending I had hoped for. The final round was yet to come. I didn't know then that the honor of the knockout blow was being reserved for me.

Over the next two months, things were quiet in the

house but strange events continued to occur in the basement. By then it was cold and the gas furnace along with the wood furnace were running. During the winter I generally spend a lot of time in my large basement workshop as well as tending to the wood furnace. One evening I was in the basement, and as I went to enter the furnace room from my workshop I found an old bucket had been placed in the middle of the doorway. As I walked back to the adjacent coal room (where I keep the wood for the furnace) I found a white handkerchief lying on top of the wood pile. A pruning pole had also been pulled down from the ceiling of the room where I kept it.

This was the week before Thanksgiving, and Fr. Mike came by to celebrate Mass in the living room. Lesa and Bobby attended with me. That night I fell asleep in bed praying the rosary and awoke to find that the cross had been removed. I later found it lying on the floor across the room. After that there were no signs of the demon spirit until Christmas when the pull chain in the closet was meticulously interlaced to form a figure eight hanging from the light. I might also note that since it was Christmastime the space was obviously empty of the Christmas decorations.

Fr. Mike checked in with me in January, and I reported that I continued to experience strange events in the basement, but one night the stench did manage to invade our bedroom and remained there for a couple hours.

It was the first week in February 2006, Lesa and I had been gone for several days attending the Super Bowl in Detroit (Steelers 21, Seahawks 10). About two weeks later, while in the basement, I saw for the first time the fleeting image of the black figure pass right in front of me as I was bending down to make some adjustments to the hot water heater. I contacted Fr. Mike and asked that we have Mass in my basement workshop soon, and he agreed. Reflecting back to Barb's vision, I deduced that this thing was now to some degree confined to the basement. I hoped that this could be the final confrontation that I had waited so long for.

The date was Friday, February 24, 2006, and Fr. Mike arrived at 5:30 P.M. to celebrate the Mass. Kerry also attended and asked if he could bring along a friend who is a missionary to the tribes of New Guinea. He was very familiar with the issues surrounding evil spirits and wanted to attend. I had cleaned up my workshop and had the boys carry the altar table down the steps where I set the room up like a small chapel with folding chairs. Along with Kerry and his missionary friend, Lesa, Bobby, and David also attended.

Our dog, Sandy, had been upstairs barking at the top of the steps until Lesa went up and brought him down, and he sat with us peacefully throughout the Mass. He seemed to know what was going on and didn't want to be excluded—he was family, too!

As Fr. Mike began the Mass there was a very distinctive tapping on the old plank wall that divided the workshop from the furnace room. We were all now used to such manifestations that would cause a chill to pass through others. I sensed the thing was weakened considerably and had played its entire hand but was still malevolent nonetheless. This intermittent tapping continued until the scripture reading and then resumed throughout the consecration portion of the Mass:

Take this, all of you, and eat it: this is my body which will be given up for you.

Take this all of you, and drink from it: this is the cup of my blood, the blood of the new and everlasting covenant.

It will be shed for you and for all men so that sins may be forgiven.

Do this in memory of me.

Through him, with him, in him, in the unity of the Holy Spirit,

All glory and honor is yours, almighty Father, for ever and ever.

I distinctly felt the thing was standing in the doorway to the furnace room watching us at a distance, but it didn't have the power to do anything other than watch. After Mass, Kerry spoke up and independently expressed the same feeling and said that he had actually seen the dim black, hazy outline of a figure standing there. As we continued to talk after the Mass was concluded, Sandy the dog slowly walked into the furnace room and then back to the coal room and sat down and did one of his "terminal stares" as I called them. I knew immediately what he was staring at; I had seen this look many times before and had caught something of what he saw on film.

Thank God, good ole Sandy had tracked the thing down and it was cornered in the coal room. It was time for it to go, I thought. This thing was ready to finally be taken down.

As I entered the room and began to talk, my voice took on the same commanding tone that it had many times before when I was in the presence of the demon and had a strange deep, ringing echo to it. This is it, I thought. After months, years, it's going to kill me or it's going to be done; only one of us is coming out of this room.

I called to Fr. Mike, "It's in this room now, Father, cowering in the corner, an extremely faint black smoky figure in the corner."

Fr. Mike then entered with his St. Benedict's crucifix and we both began to pray aloud simultaneously. He prayed:

Loving God we praise and thank you for your mercy and love, your healing power, your deliverance and freedom from the evil. We take the authority you have given us over the power of darkness and rebuke Satan in Jesus' name and Beelzebub and all the demons and all the forces of evil that seek to control and attack this house and property and the Cranmer Family.

Jesus Christ come against you, with the power of God, with the angels and saints behind us, we command you in the name of Jesus Christ to leave these premises, you have no rights or authority here, this house belongs to God, it is sanctified by prayer, by the celebration of Mass, by the holiness of the people here. By the power of God we cast you into the darkness where you belong, never to return.

"Demon, this is the end," I kept repeating loudly. "You will leave now. In the name of Jesus Christ this is over. In the blessed name of Jesus and his shed blood, YOU WILL LEAVE AND LEAVE NOW! This is my house. We will not leave. You will leave and be cast into the abyss! All of the turmoil and death that you have caused in this house will also leave with you. THIS IS OVER!"

I felt and could sense the black entity, the black misty figure, melting right into the floor before us. A fire that had once blazed and engulfed the house, each room, had now burnt itself out, and we were stepping on and extinguishing its final, feeble smoking embers! All that had occurred in the house, the blood, the death, the anguish, was swirling around it as if going down a large bloody drain.

I wish I could report that there was a clap of thunder or some impressive display as this now weakened pitiful thing left, but fortunately it no longer could muster the strength to manage blood on the walls, scratches, body blows, horrible stenches, or psychological warfare. But it certainly was enough for me to sense this once terrifying opponent, with all of its brashness and confidence, withering in weakness and finally defeated. If it could have, it surely would have struck out at us with one final blow, but it couldn't—as the power of the cross, as I always expected, had prevailed. This hideous, malevolent being that had been so bold, that had terrorized us for so long, had attacked us mentally and physically, tried to tear our family apart and kill us, was now a lump of withering remains before the cross of Jesus. As in the famous poem by T.S. Eliot this war ended "not with a bang but a whimper." This once roaring fire had been smothered. Its evil and rage had been overcome with the power of our love, and the power of God's love for us.

When we were finished praying I took the cross from the altar as all present watched and placed it in the room on the floor where the demon had just met its demise, then casually turned off the light.

"Let's go upstairs," I told everyone. I was confident that the long war with this evil entity was finally over. We all hugged one another. Together, as a family, we had endured the Hell it had thrown at us. We had won, and had Heaven to thank for it. The door to this strange parallel world was finally closed, but I would be forever changed because I knew what was on the other side of it. I still had my family, my sanity, and my faith. But most of all . . . this house was ours at last.

Father Ron Lengwin and Connie Valenti

Seven years later, November 2012

The office of the Pittsburgh Diocese is in downtown Pittsburgh not far from the famous point where the Allegheny and Monongahela rivers join to form the Ohio. It's in a tall, gray, anonymous-looking office building that could house just about any business, with only crucifixes and holy paintings on the walls to remind visitors that it's actually the home of a holy or religious institution. Fr. Lengwin, who as the vicar general is second only to the bishop in authority, has his office there, and I made an appointment to visit him with my coauthor, Erica Manfred, while writing this book. I still had many questions. I realized even though I had talked to him every day for over two years I never did fully understand where his mystical insights had come from.

My coauthor and I took the elevator up to his office and were greeted by the tall, slender, imposing figure in black clerical garb who walked rather stiffly and looked younger than his seventy-odd years. He'd recently had multiple coronary bypass surgery, but you'd never have known it from looking at him. His office is comfortable but very formal. It could be the office of any corporate executive.

Fr. Ron comes across as authoritative and all business at first, but he drops this veneer to some extent after you get to know him. He's not a warm and embracing priest like Fr. Mike or Fr. Ed, but is more reserved, intellectual, and somewhat forbidding, although he does have a very kind manner. During the interview with my coauthor he admitted that he's actually somewhat shy, which may be why he comes across as aloof. He's certainly not reluctant to talk openly about himself or his beliefs and has always been extremely helpful when it came to me and my concerns.

He got right to the heart of the matter when my coauthor asked him what he thought should be the most important message of the book.

"I think people need to know that personal evil is real in the world," he said with conviction. "People have ideas that are very wrong about demons and Lucifer. They think they're not real, that Satan is just a figment of our imagination, that he doesn't really exist. Saying that the Devil doesn't exist is a way to rationalize away the wrong that is done by us. But the good and evil we do has consequences in our life and the lives of those around us and perhaps around the world, just as we as a church believe prayer has great power.

"My favorite topic is Mystery," he continued. "Mystery as God finds a place in our life so Mystery gets extended to our life. Divine providence is how Mystery works through our life. It inspires us, heals us in ways we don't always know. I believe with St. Augustine that God loves each of us as though there is only one of us to love."

Erica then asked: "Was this situation at the Cranmer house the only one you've dealt with? Are you an exorcist?"

He explained that he wasn't an exorcist but a coordinator of the exorcism effort in the diocese when it is deemed necessary. He is aware of any request that is made from a parish, and also noted that the diocese did in fact have a priest currently in training to fill the position of "diocesan exorcist." There are also convocations for priests to discuss exorcism in the hopes of identifying additional priests and members of the laity who may want to assist.

"So often we're not dealing with possession but infestation or some other manifestation of evil where a priest can go in and not have to confront an evil spirit directly but rather pray to release that place or person from the evil," Fr. Ron told us. "For example, Fr. Mike is very well known to be one of those priests."

"I'm just gratified that although there was no specific earthly design, we wound up with an extremely effective team," I added, "with you as the advisor behind the scenes, the nuns praying, and Fr. Mike and Fr. Ed being there on the ground." I recalled Fr. Mike's tacit resentment that Fr. Ron didn't come to the house but obviously didn't want to mention it.

"After months had gone by and we hadn't been able to overcome what was happening in the house the bishop asked me to assess whether a formal exorcism was needed," Fr. Ron informed us.

I told him that what had always amazed me was the backstory and details about the house he revealed to me, and that I had been able to verify at least 90 percent of what he had said occurred in the past, or was going to happen. This is when he dropped the bombshell I never expected. He told us that it was not he who had provided all of the details about the house. Someone named Connie Valenti had given him much of the information he had passed on to me. I had no idea who she was, even though I happened to have met her several times at Christmas parties held at the home of Fr. Ron's sister after the events I've described in my house came to an end. In fact on one occasion she came up to Lesa and commented, "Things are a lot better in your house now, aren't they, dear?" Lesa told her yes, things were better, but had no idea how she knew about the house, other than Fr. Ron confiding in her. At the time it seemed a little odd that she knew about our situation, because Fr. Ron is not the type who reveals confidences.

"We worked together very closely on your case," Fr. Ron explained, describing her as an extremely gifted Catholic intuitive. "She had more specific knowledge about the doctor and everything related to the family who built and first lived in the house. If you open a pathway to the past she can walk down it and relate what she sees. She grew up as a child believing everyone talked to God, because she did, so she was surprised when she found out not everyone has the same insights she does."

Erica asked if she considered herself a "psychic."

"No, absolutely not, she will not be described as or even relate to being 'a psychic,'" Fr. Ron said emphatically.

"She's a deeply spiritual person who doesn't want to be called a psychic or medium and doesn't think she deserves the term mystic. She prefers to just be called an 'intuitive.'"

He told us they had a long history together. He met Connie when he was a young priest, when a mutual friend told him he should talk to her and ask her what she could tell him about himself.

"When we first spoke on the phone I didn't tell her who I was," Fr. Ron revealed. "She said that she saw me dressed in black and asked if I was a priest." She also said, 'I see a long cable.' I had no idea what she was talking about but soon I became the chairperson of a committee that brought cable television to Pittsburgh.

"It all started from there," Fr. Ron explained. "I thought, God's trying to tell me something. My conversations with her opened my mind up to the many ways God can communicate with us. Certain people, Christian mystics, can see things and communicate at a very deep level."

"Why then was this woman so reluctant to talk to me directly or let her name be known?" I asked.

"Many years ago Connie's insights brought her a lot of unwelcome attention from the press and others," Fr. Ron revealed. "So she retreated into private life until she started working with me on your case. She's very secretive about her talents."

He explained that her gifts originally focused on an amazing ability to see illnesses. She actually would see people as silhouettes with an orange spot wherever they were sick. Word of mouth about her remarkable gift spread until she even had doctors calling her. Then the police called, and wanting to do all she could to help,

Connie worked with them. This backfired badly. Forty years ago she was highly publicized in the Pittsburgh newspapers as helping the police with the investigation of several high-profile murders. Requests started to pour in and she was even offered money to reveal the past and foretell the future. She never accepted money for her information, returning checks that were sent to her. Criminals started calling, which terrified her.

Her mother and her brother, who is a prominent attorney, became very upset. Some of her neighbors began to refer to her as "the witch," and that was the final straw for this devotedly religious woman. She withdrew and kept her "gifts" to herself from that point forward, that is until she was approached by Fr. Ron about our house.

"Public opinion concerning these gifts was very different then," Fr. Ron explained. "It was all seen as superstitious hokum that should be avoided. I went to see her mother and became very close to her and her family. I advised her to stop taking phone calls for her 'visions' since the backlash was becoming quite serious. I don't know that God sent me to her to protect her but it seems like He did. I helped her and Connie helped me as well. We eventually wound up writing a column together for the *Pittsburgh Catholic* called 'Home Again.' When it was suggested that I do a call-in radio program I didn't think that I could do it because I'm an introvert, but Connie encouraged me. I've been on the air every week for thirty-eight years now."

Fr. Ron then described how he'd used her gifts on his radio show for years. He'd have a guest scheduled, give Connie the topic, she'd say a short prayer, and then she'd tell a story based on the life of Christ that would fit the topic. They would eventually write a book together called *Stories of Jesus: A Gospel of Faith and Imagination*. It relates various stories from the life of Jesus that do not appear specifically in the scriptures, but Connie sees them as they occurred, and they are all quite believable, compelling, and scripturally sound. They also bring a deep peace of mind to the reader.

When Fr. Ron was directed by the bishop (now Cardinal Wuerl) to get involved with the issues at my house he called Connie initially and she immediately had extremely strong visions and insights as to what had occurred there over the decades.

"I'd relay all of her insights to you," he said. "However it happened—inspiration or enlightenment—I'd also be able to tell you things that I saw happening before or after what she revealed—but her visions were always at the core. She not only saw what happened long ago, she also saw you and your family coming to the house to eventually expunge the evil. She saw you as a little boy and knew that you were anointed in some way to fight the battle. She also felt her gifts were directed to assist you in this undertaking."

"Wow," was all I could say in response to these new revelations. When I had absorbed what he'd told me, I asked, "Fr. Mike always conjectured that the issues in the house may also be connected to the land that it is built upon, that something happened there long before the house was built. Could you at some point ask

Connie if she sees anything predating the house? We've heard various stories about the old oak tree in the front yard, that it has something to do with Colonial times and possibly George Washington who owned land in the area. But could Fr. Mike be correct, could there be more evil to the story than we already know?"

At this point Fr. Ron astounded me by simply picking up the phone and calling Connie. "Let's ask her," he said.

I was stunned. I never expected to actually speak to this mysterious person whom I'd just found out had played such a significant role in the whole process. After a few minutes of introductions and light conversation, Fr. Ron got right to the point and asked her directly if there was anything significant about the land that the house was built upon.

Connie's voice was just as ordinary as her presence, the comforting voice of a motherly older woman with a typical Pittsburgh accent. She wasn't the least bit pretentious. She laughed when something struck her funny, and her laugh came easily. However, when asked a question she became serious and wasn't vague at all about what she saw. She was very detailed, focused, and specific about the origin of the evil in our house.

"When the earth was created there were fallen angels," she explained. "Followers of the great angel who rebelled and became the god of this world of darkness. There were many powerful angels who admired Lucifer and wanted to be like him. They were eventually all cast out from the presence of the Almighty and fell to earth. These followers of Satan now roam the earth and cause all types of evil. They can also take possession of places and dwellings for various reasons. That was the case with your house and the land it's on.

"Some terrible evil deeds took place there long ago. In addition to all of the illegal abortions, many of which were late term and caused the death of the child and sometimes the mother, there was much suffering perpetrated upon women and children on your property. Before the house was built, long before, I see a mother screaming, covered in blood, screaming for her three daughters who were killed right in front of her. She was killed as well, and I see her still there, in the yard screaming for her lost children."

"Were the murders committed by Indians?" I asked.

Connie replied, "I see the spirits. I see one man in particular with a big knife. There was a massacre of the mother and her three children by Native Americans who were angry at their land being invaded by settlers. The husband wasn't there when it occurred; he came home to find this grizzly scene. One of his daughters, the youngest one, lived until the next day but died from loss of blood. He buried his family right there in the yard where it took place. He took a sapling tree and planted it over their graves as a memorial to them. The tree took nourishment from their bodies and today is a huge oak tree. Sometimes at night, when all is still and quiet, one can faintly hear the wails of this poor woman, crying for her lost family. I believe that the evil spirits associated with this massacre certainly could have remained attached to this plot of land and their goal has been to destroy and terrorize young children. These demons were later further energized by a curse placed on the house when it was built and then worked to cause the evil deeds that eventually took place in the house after it was built. In the Cranmer house and on the land there was not only the demon spirit, but many captive human souls who remained as spirits or ghosts.

"On several occasions," she continued, "Father and I would pray and I would go into the house through my mind, I would see things, things from the past that happened there. Father and I would pray about it. I was concerned about your family, the children specifically. They don't understand. Little ones are more open to seeing evil and being hurt by it because they don't have the ability to shut their minds like adults do. Children can't; they are intellectually so innocent and vulnerable.

"The house was filled with departed children. There were also some spirits of their poor mothers as well, lamenting their lost children. A lot of terrible things happened in that house and on the land besides the deaths, and evil possessed the house as its own. The evil owned the house, and it emanated from the house. When Bob came to buy it he was divinely prepared to eventually deal with the evil and all that it did and represented. He would not be run over by it nor forced out by it. He had the strength and was going to confront it and nothing was going to push him away. That's rare because most people would have moved."

"But why was I the one 'supernaturally' drawn to this house? That's my primary question. Why was I compelled or 'led' to this house to get involved with this whole mess? To take on this fight?" I asked, still puzzled by that question.

"Do you really want to know?" she asked.

"Yes," I said, not sure that I really did.

"You were killed there in that house and you were the one chosen to come back." Then she quickly added to reassure me, "But you should know you were loved. She was a young girl under a lot of influences to make her situation go away. It was a different time. It wasn't that she didn't love you; she was forced into it due to the pressures of time and propriety.

"There were many girls," Connie continued. "I know all their stories. Some of the women who came in and out of your house were very tough, some were very frightened, some felt that they had no choice. There were a lot of different energies in that house over the years. It's unbelievable. It fills the whole house up. They want their stories told, so I've started to write them down."

To tell the truth, I was blown away by this information. She had struck a nerve about something that only I knew, something that I had kept to myself over the years. "I'd like to know about the young woman with the long black hair," I asked her. I'd never told anyone about the spirit I thought of as the "woman in the white dress" before. She had appeared to me a number of times, sometimes in dreams and other times I wasn't sure. She would just be there. I had a strong attraction to her and was extremely curious about her.

"With the white dress," Connie said. "She's beautiful, even gorgeous."

"I feel that I know her," I said.

"Her mind was way beyond her years," Connie said.

"She was very educated. She wanted a family but accidently got pregnant before she was married."

"Was this the woman who died during an abortion?" I asked.

"Yes."

"I know that," I told her. "I've seen her not so much in apparition form. I've seen her in my dreams as I slept. She's come into the room and stood beside the bed."

"She died at the foot of your stairs in the foyer. She was taken to a hospital but it was too late. She had been sent to the doctor by a close friend of her family. He was a prominent Pittsburgh politician who possibly had her taken there to get the abortion." Connie spoke with sadness in her voice.

This new information was a little too much for me to accept, and I must say that I'm still extremely skeptical and apprehensive about buying into the reincarnation theory. But Connie did know about this woman with the long black hair, "the woman in white." At the time I thought this woman might be just another demonic trick to screw with my mind, and rationally I still lean that way, but Connie was correct about so much, it's hard not to wonder if there isn't something to it.

She had hit upon some personal thoughts for me. "Connie," I said, moved by all I'd heard, "for me sitting here talking to you after so many years of this, I have such a feeling of relief. Obviously you've touched on something that only I know. In a way a lot more makes sense now. I don't know how many times I was with my children on Christmas morning opening presents and I would walk out of the room and a door would be ajar, or things would be thrown down the steps, like someone was extremely sad or even angry that they couldn't participate."

"There were a lot of little children whose lives were snuffed out," Connie explained. "They were watching. All those that have passed in that house want their story told but the evil was holding them captive, but now that the evil has departed they have gone to the light. But I believe that the woman in white is still there; she doesn't want to leave you."

Father Ron interrupted. "In order to know the whole story you'd have to believe in the possibility of reincarnation, which is contrary to the teachings of the Church. This beautiful woman was possibly Bob's mother in a previous life and that's the attraction. Am I close?" Father Ron asked her. "She was somehow trapped there and was calling out to him?"

"Yes," Connie responded. "Many times evil spirits will pretend to be something or someone that they are not, but that is not the case here, this woman is not evil, that's all I can say. There are a lot of good people who haven't crossed over. Once this story gets out your house will have a different feel.

"I can tell you this," she went on, "Heaven wants everything exposed that happened in this house, all of the sorrow, and the terrible deeds. Evil is real and I do believe this book will help people understand it's not their imagination, these things do happen."

After we left I was somewhat unnerved by the whole experience. It was a lot of information for me to process. Like I said, I wasn't sure about the story of the young woman. I thought that it had been a trick by the evil entity to further confuse me, but then Connie had been accurate about so many minute details, and it all did seem to fit the puzzle. I'd asked Connie the name and identity of the woman in white, but she said the woman didn't want it known, so that would have to remain a mystery. The time wasn't right for me to be told.

I'm still puzzled by it, can't say that I fully believe it, but it is intriguing. Was I really drawn back to the house because I was terminated there in a previous life? Christianity absolutely doesn't believe in any form of reincarnation, but many cultures and religions do, as supposedly did some early Christians. I'm sure we'll all find out someday.

What intrigued me the most from my conversation with Connie was the story of the massacre. I thought I could do some research and find something on record about it.

The following weekend I decided to dive into the Internet and find out as much about the land and its history as I could. I hoped to discover information about it in military records from the time period. So I did some thorough investigating and what I found astonished me. Brownsville Road was originally a colonial trail linking Fort Pitt, at the headwaters of the Ohio River (Pittsburgh), to Redstone Fort (Brownsville), on Nemacolin's Trail, originally a Native American path that crossed the Allegheny Mountains. This trail eventually became known as "the National Road," one of the first U.S. highways (later U.S. 40). Thus Brownsville Road became a major road link between Pittsburgh and all points south. The land upon which the house sits was officially surveyed as a separate tract of 689 acres on November 1, 1787.

The owners of the land were Samuel and Robert Purviance, a distinguished Huguenot Irish merchant family of Baltimore who were active purveyors of supplies needed by the Continental Army during the Revolution. I'm certain that neither of these two prominent and distinguished gentlemen ever settled here, as the land was possibly given in payment of government debt. It was probably rented out in parcels. However, Samuel Purviance was captured and murdered by a band of Native Americans while traveling through the region to Kentucky in 1788. Trouble with the natives began at the conclusion of the Revolution when the British ceded what became the Northwest Territory to the United States. On August 7, 1789, President George Washington signed the Northwest Ordinance into law, creating the new territory south of the Great Lakes, north and west of the Ohio River, and east of the Mississippi River.

This land was now open to mass settlement; in fact it was encouraged by the government, which sold the land as a major source of revenue. The British previously forbade settlement on this land, and even though they controlled it to an extent, the eleven or so Native American tribes saw themselves as the rightful owners because they considered it their tribal lands. They certainly had not been party to the Treaty of Paris, which transferred its control to the new American government. Thus as the British had probably foreseen, the United States soon had a new war on its hands.

The Northwest Indian War was a brutal affair that began in 1785 but really heated up around 1790, and that's where history intersects with our story. The war, which had been primarily in Ohio, did make its way into Pennsylvania, and in 1791 Ft. Pitt was repaired and regarrisoned. This war was the first major military event of the new U.S. government, and a major crisis for President George Washington. Although nineteenth-century Indian wars are much more notable in American history, the Northwest Indian War produced more casualties for the United States Army and noncombatants than the combined battles of Geronimo, Crazy Horse, Sitting Bull, and Cochise. In the first major battle the American Indians achieved their highest rate of casualties against the U.S. Army ever recorded.

In looking for any stories related to Indian raids in the area during the late 1700s, I found a letter deep in the archives of the U.S. War Department. It was dated March 31, 1792, and was basically a one-page report dispatched from the commander of Ft. Pitt, Isaac Craig, to the secretary of war, Henry Knox. In the closing paragraph he states he was recently informed *that the Indians have killed the wife and three children of a Deliverance Brown—Brown having escaped by being some distance from the house.* Even though there are no longer records of the place names used, this occurred in the general vicinity of the fort. Now the chance of all of these facts coming together so specifically defies coincidence. And few had probably even read that one-page letter since the day that it was written in 1792.

Historical writings are clear that in the decades leading

up to this Indian uprising women and children were generally taken hostage by the Indians for ransom, or just taken to become part of the tribe (as chronicled in the famous story of Mary Jemison). However, in this war "terror" apparently was the primary weapon against settlers, and the Indians used it with striking efficiency and boldness on the doorsteps of a major fort.

Certainly the Native Americans were fighting to expel invaders and didn't see themselves as aggressors but as defending what was rightfully theirs. There were many atrocities committed by white settlers against them as well.

It also made me stop and think that over the years I had literally covered the walls of the house with a collection of prints and paintings of Indian warriors from the same period. What had driven me to do so? I had even developed something of a passion for it and I wasn't sure why. I had never had any deep interest in American Indians, but I started my collection a few years after we moved in and continued for the next twenty years. Could these events of long ago not only have been resonating in the house, but in me as well? And was this land still claimed by the evil that had been described by Connie and consummated in the front yard?

To verify the facts of the massacre, I decided to actually look for proof of the existence of a grave on my property, under the old oak tree. As the newspaper article that opened this book reported, I found such a grave with the help of both ancient and modern technology. I used an old dowsing technique for finding buried objects that I saw on the History Channel. I held two copper rods and walked around until they moved indicating the grave at the oak tree, and then hired a company to use ground-penetrating radar to confirm my finding. The resulting report stated that there is a large area of "disturbed ground" exactly where Connie and the rods said the grave was. It's the right size and shape, and appears to contain four figures lying horizontally four to six feet down. I was obviously astonished and told the local newspaper. The story caused widespread interest in Pittsburgh, especially from schoolchildren. But for me it simply confirmed that Connie was right—*once again*.

Update on the Cranmer Family, Blue Room, Brentwood, and Bob, 2013

JESSICA, 29

Jessica never became the lawyer I hoped she would become, but then I personally wouldn't want to be an attorney, either. Like so many, her marriage ended in divorce and she's now a single mother with two young sons, Collin and Thomas. However, she is making a good living and went to school to learn medical office administration. I'm extremely proud of her. Collin is now twelve, very bright and well behaved in school. He spends a lot of time with his friends at the Brentwood Library and loves to watch the WWE. Although he is guarded with his emotions, I don't see any lingering damage or effects from his early childhood experiences.

BOBBY, 28

As one might expect, Bobby has had the hardest time since the events of the book. He's had his share of extreme highs and even lower lows. He's married and has two children (Ryliegh—4 and Noah—2) but has struggled off and on with depression and unemployment associated with the construction business. Currently he is on the upswing, has found God, and has a lot to look forward to. He is pursuing a career in commercial construction doing project inspection and management. He is extremely perceptive and intelligent, and has a great future ahead of him, I'm certain.

DAVID, 26

David is still a responsible, solid young man and continues to amaze me with his independence. He finished his enlistment in the Marine Corps after serving an assignment in Iraq. He is married and his wife is a registered nurse. They have a daughter (Jayden—3) and a beautiful home. He works in the heating and air-conditioning industry. He is still deeply concerned about the plight of others and was recently featured on a local TV news segment for his volunteer work installing a free furnace for a poor family.

CHARLIE, 25

Charlie is doing extremely well considering all that he's been through. He's a licensed massage therapist and plans to move into physical therapy. His fiancée is a brilliant girl who is studying and working in the marine biology field. They now live in Florida. He is an accomplished musician on several instruments, writes songs and hopes to pursue music as a part-time career as well. He has no lingering or lasting effects from his experiences in the house and has a solid, practical disposition and personality.

LESA, 52

Lesa continues to be my trusted right arm in everything I do. I started a business five years ago and she now works as my office manager, which includes all of the financials, and she does a wonderful job. She gained a lot of weight during our ordeal but has since dropped over eighty-five pounds and goes to the gym three times a week. We bought our country home on a little river in northwestern Pennsylvania, built a barn, have one horse so far, and plan to retire there at some point.

THE BLUE ROOM

This room is still blue with the original wallpaper, which I purposely didn't take down when we recovered the rest of the house. I want it to be a memorial to what happened there and also the evil that was overcome. Lesa and I made it our bedroom again in 2006, and I can say that it is the most peaceful room in the house. The kids agree; one of our grandchildren loves to fall off to sleep in our big bed with the fireplace burning—alone!

BRENTWOOD, 2013

The town has undergone a peaceful change over the past few years. Even though there was a racial incident at the high school that made the national news in 2012, and a president of the town council was arrested for fraud in 2007, the police department is now under solid leadership and is the professional force I always wanted to see.

In another positive development, a solid guy who was on my staff and then subsequently deputy-director of economic development for the county was just elected mayor. I have great hopes for the borough's future under his leadership.

MY PERSONAL JOURNEY

For a few years after the events ceased I suffered from a form of PTSD, always on edge, always looking for signs of the demon's return. To a lesser degree it remains to this day. Last summer, when some strange-looking fluid turned up on a lightbulb I rushed it off to a lab for analysis. I was relieved to discover that it turned out to be melted plastic.

As to my faith, all of my beliefs are not as cut-and-dried as they previously were. We do live in a world akin to *The Matrix*, but I didn't find playing the role of Neo or Mr. Anderson exciting. I smile when I hear ministers or priests preaching as if they have it all figured out. Likewise, the same goes for academics and scientists with their patronizing attitudes about the nonexistence of the supernatural, that the here and now is all there is. Science and religion have merely scratched the surface in unraveling the reality of our existence.

I primarily wrote this book as a witness that pure evil does exist apart from the intentions and flawed characteristics of human beings—that it can be openly and aggressively malevolent, working to oppress or even on rare occasions possess individuals, causing them to do evil things in the process. But ultimately I feel privileged to have been given the opportunity to experience the supernatural firsthand—to understand that demons, angels, Jesus, the Devil all exist just as described. I've seen it, smelled it, and witnessed their power. My faith has been verified and confirmed just as if I'd seen Jesus walking on the water, feeding the five thousand, or raising a person from the dead—it's all real. The Bible states, "For unto whomsoever much is given, of him shall be much required." That is why I had to write this book. I had to tell the story.

When you pass through the waters, I will be with you;
and when you pass through the rivers, they will not
sweep over you. When you walk through the fire,
you will not be burned; the flames will not set you
ablaze. For I am the Lord thy God, the holy
one of Israel, your Savior . . .
—BOOK OF ISAIAH, NIV 43:2-3, 690 B.C.

APPENDIX

Demons have been around since the creation of the world. Satan and his minions are described in the Bible, and there is a whole body of scholarly research about them, which gives credence to the events of this book. We felt that a section on demonology was warranted to give readers insight into the religious background behind this story. Adam Blai, who came to the house and participated in the events related in this book, is a scholar and demonologist who trains priests in how to deal with demonic infestation and possession. I was fortunate to learn much of this information directly from him and want you the reader to have the benefit of what I learned through his extensive research on the subject.

The following Fundamental Information and Q & A are taken from religiousdemonology.com by Adam C. Blai, Peritus, M.S.:

FUNDAMENTAL INFORMATION

1. The spiritual world is legalistic. There are rules just like there are laws in our world. God wrote the laws and God enforces them.

2. Usually we break the rules and through our free will allow evil spirits to start affecting us. When it is simply allowed by God it is usually to encourage our spiritual growth or show us the reality of the spiritual world. In the midst of things it's hard to see this but usually after a short period of problems a lifetime of spiritual growth follows.

3. Spiritual "legal rights" can be given to evil spirits, people, buildings, objects, or family lines.

    Possession is the most famous example, being full rights to the body of a person and therefore ability to take over their body. Rights of that level are almost always explicitly given by the person, usually in exchange for something. Rights to oppress a person are usually given by spirit communication, the occult, or black magic.

    Rights to a building are usually given through the rule breaking that goes on there, or through explicit permission from the person with authority over the building. When we bless a home with the owners' request we mark that territory for God. The opposite happens with black magic and serious violations of God's rules. Rights to a building usually leads to infestation by evil spirits. Once they are in through free will they have to be cast out and then the home has to be claimed for God.

    Rights to an object is a common way that people involved in black magic get spirits into a person's home or life. They cast "spells" on an object that give rights to evil spirits to attach to it. Then they try to get the target to accept the item as a gift, etc. Then through free will the person has brought a spirit into their life. Sometimes they simply break in and leave the object hidden in a home; sometimes they leave it behind after a visit.

Rights to a family line are usually given in multi-generational cults that serve evil spirits. Usually these spirits try very hard to stay with the family once they are in, often afflicting the next generation starting a few years before their current host will likely die.

4. Spiritual rights to a person can be limited, taking the form of having spirits in them, but not having them take over their body. This generally takes the form of spirits residing in the body, felt by the person at times and felt violently during prayer over them. This requires the sacramental life and deliverance work, not an exorcism. It is not uncommon for people with spirits in them to have untreatable medical conditions that stop as soon as the spirit is cast out.

5. There is often a mental health component to situations with spiritual affliction. It is normal to be frustrated and possibly depressed after being harassed by spirits for some time. It's also not uncommon for spirits to cause physical health problems if they are inside of a person.

6. Once rights are obtained by evil spirits they do not give them up without being forced to. They may make it seem like they will but it's a lie. The rights must be renounced and then prayer must be said to cast out/away the spirit. Prayers to fill the space occupied by the evil spirits with the Holy Spirit should follow. This could take the form of a baptism in the Holy Spirit, a house blessing, etc.

7. The breaking of rights and casting out/away of evil spirits is generally referred to as "spiritual warfare"

or deliverance work. Deliverance prayers should only be used by someone trained and approved to do so. Catholic laity are not to pray "over" (or lay hands on) another person; they can pray for that person only. There are exceptions to this when someone has been deemed to have a charism for deliverance work and has permission. A special ritual within the Catholic Church, called exorcism, is done by priests with the permission of their bishop for cases of full possession only.

8. Assuming that you are Christian or Catholic your first contact should be your local pastor or minister. You may find that you cannot find someone willing to work with you to determine if a spiritual problem is present and pray against it. If that is the case you may need to reach out to your bishop's office directly.

9. There are cases that are simply mental illness that are mistaken for spiritual problems. Unfortunately serious mental illness can cause a state where a person is convinced they are possessed or that the voices they are hearing are spirits. It takes experience and evaluation by someone trained in mental health to identify these cases. It is imperative that medical and psychiatric situations not go untreated because the spiritual hypothesis has been accepted inappropriately.

10. Many Christian and Catholic parishes have prayer meetings or people that pray deliverance prayers. There are many people who call themselves demonologists or exorcists. It is important to verify that they have been trained and have a calling to this work, usually through their church (bishop's office).

QUESTIONS AND ANSWERS

Q: **What makes you qualified to write on possession, exorcism, and hauntings?**

A: As professional background I have a Master of Science degree in adult clinical psychology. I've worked for over seven years as a therapist in both community and forensic settings. I've done hundreds of psychological evaluations and worked with all of the extremes of mental illness and human evil.

My spiritual work is within the Roman Catholic Church, and I work under obedience to bishops from a number of dioceses. My authority to teach priests comes from my being named a peritus of religious demonology and exorcism by formal decree of my bishop. I am also an auxiliary member of the International Association of Exorcists where I've learned from the most experienced exorcists in the world.

My current functions include training priests in exorcism and deliverance on a national level, psychological evaluations to help determine if cases are mundane or demonic, assisting at exorcisms and house blessings, performing deliverance prayers, counseling victims and family members, investigating claims of paranormal activity, and speaking to the public about the dangers of paranormal investigating.

Q: **What is a religious demonologist?**

A: The term demonology simply means the study of demons. The popular term demonologist is therefore a person who studies demons. A religious demonologist is someone who studies demons from a religious perspective. The title "religious demonologist" is generally granted by the Church and usually requires a Ph.D. on demonology.

Functionally a religious demonologist evaluates people or places that have possibly become entangled with the demonic and assists at religious intervention against demons.

There has been a recent trend of people claiming to be demonologists on the Internet and in paranormal television shows. Though these people might be well trained by exorcists and have access to the verbal tradition passed down through mentorship under exorcists, it is unlikely. There are very few lay people admitted to the inner world of exorcism and demonology. Anyone claiming to help people with demonic problems from a Catholic perspective, or especially to be a religious demonologist, should be able to prove that they work under the authority of a bishop and with exorcists.

Q: **What is a demon?**

A: A demon is a fallen angel that rebelled against God along with Lucifer, refusing to be humble before, and serve, God.

A demon is an immortal spiritual entity that hates human beings with a complete and merciless passion. Their only goal for humans is to deceive and corrupt them into turning away from God so that they die in a poor spiritual state and become their eternal slave and victim.

Q: **Do you do solemn exorcisms?**

A: No, never. A solemn exorcism can only be performed by a priest with permission from their bishop. Laity should never attempt to perform a solemn exorcism.

I assist at exorcisms, which usually means I hold the possessed person and respond to the prayers in the ritual. I may also help by giving advice about the exorcism as part of training.

Q: **If I say a demon's name will it attack me or possess me?**

A: Very likely no.

There seems to be a common myth that saying a demon's name causes an immediate reaction from said demon. There must be two factors in place before a demon attacks a person: an interest on the part of Hell to attack the person and some "rights" to attack them recognized by God (so the demon has permission to attack them from God). If demons attacked every person that said their name many people a day would be attacked by the Devil for saying "Satan."

Conversely, not saying a demon's name does not stop it from attacking a person. People that are being attacked and call for help almost never know what is bothering them and very likely have not said its name.

Q: **Knowing or saying a demon's name gives me power over it, right?**

A: No, only God has power over demons.

This belief may come from the fact that the Roman Ritual for exorcism involves trying to get a demon's name in order to make the exorcism more effective. The power of an exorcism comes from God; knowing the name has some benefit to the process but is not part of every successful exorcism.

People not called to spiritual warfare who know a demon's name have no more "power over" that demon than a high school student has power over a professional boxer in the ring just because he knows that boxer's name.

Having "power" or "authority" are dangerous ideas because they inflate the ego and lead people to pride about their imagined greatness. This is exactly what the Devil wants because then they are likely to overstep their bounds. The Devil's first sin was pride and it is a great human weakness and therefore he often tricks people into shifting the respect and credit due to God toward mortals who have no intrinsic power or authority without Jesus. We do have authority over demons when we invoke the name of Jesus, but it is Jesus, not us, that affects the demons.

Q: **Are Satan and the demons in Hell?**
A: No.

The Book of Revelation is clear that after the war in Heaven Lucifer and the errant angels were cast down to earth to roam here and tempt mankind until the final judgment. It seems to be a common assumption or misunderstanding that demons are locked in Hell; they are not. When demons are cast out of a person or location they are usually tortured by Satan for their failure and then reassigned to a new case. We know this from encountering the same demons over time in disparate locations and times.

Q: **Can demons possess anyone at any time?**
A: No.

Demons can scare people and influence their feelings, and sometimes thoughts, for a short time. Possession requires people to explicitly give permission. It is also very important to remember that demons don't move an inch without permission from God; they are not running free. God does not wish demons to harm people, but He doesn't violate our free will if we choose to form a relationship with demons.

Q: **What about "X" religion and demons?**
A: I can't really know the answer to that.

I take a Catholic perspective and my experience is with using Catholic prayers, symbols, sacramentals, and rituals against demons. I cannot ethically speak to whether other religious perspectives work or don't, because I have not witnessed them. I would not expect that God's mercy would be withheld from those acting in good faith to help another person no matter the religion they practice.

Q: **If my faith is strong am I safe to confront demons?**
A: Very likely no.

Faith is not enough to make one safe and effective in confronting demons. First one should be working under the authority, and therefore protection, of the Church. Practically this means under a bishop's authority and direction. There are also specific gifts of God's grace moving through exorcists and others in this work that protect them from feeling fear, being driven mad, or being injured. Only people called by God to have direct interactions with evil spirits are equipped with these gifts of protection and efficacy; faith does not make God give these gifts. We see that bishops are moved by the Holy Spirit to appoint those chosen by God for this work.

Q: **How do I become a demonologist?**

A: Why would you want to?

Many people in the paranormal community, and in the public, seem to think demonology is "cool" or "exciting" or will make them famous. These reasons fade very quickly for those who actually meet a demon.

Being a demonologist is a spiritual calling that leads one to live part of their life in nightmare environments of intense physical, emotional, and spiritual suffering that people go through. People don't choose to be demonologists or exorcists; God makes people demonologists or exorcists.

Q: **What are some common tricks of the demonic?**

A: The most common is appearing to be a helpful or needy spirit/ghost/phenomenon/guide.

The enemy almost never appears in their true form; they lie and deceive constantly. Many cases of demonic oppression and possession start with a "harmless" or "helpful" spirit interaction.

They sometimes start with communication with what seems to be a dearly departed relative or helpful spirit guide, or a pitiful soul that needs help. If demons showed up and looked horrible and menacing people would run the other way and right into a church. They reel people in slowly by offering knowledge, playing on pity, giving comfort or power. Only when they have a sufficient hold will their true intent (to take people away from God and destroy them) become clear.

Another is convincing people that they will give life, health, power, money, fame, sex, etc.

The enemy often takes advantage of weakness or misfortune: They come when people are sick, bankrupt, depressed, or swollen with pride. They offer to fix problems or elevate one above others. The trick comes later when the person is at their peak and they tear it all down so that they suffer the most intensely.

Another is tricking people into letting a "spirit" enter their body.

The enemy has many tricks for convincing people to let a spirit into their body. Using the body as a tool to "free" or "remove" a spirit or demon from a haunted location is one.

There is always an act of free will involved in letting a demon enter the body; one just might be unaware that it is a demon. Permission might be given in response to a deception, but the door is opened nonetheless. One should never assume that they can get something out once it is let in. Entering the body is not the same as possession, but it is a large step.

Q: **How is free will granted for full possession to take place?**

A: A person makes a clear choice to say yes, verbally or in their mind, to the demon's explicit request to fully possess them, knowing full well what they are giving themselves over to.

Q: **Can demon possession really do the horrible things to the human body seen in movies?**

A: Hollywood exaggerates things, and not all phenomena happen in each case. Bodies do sometimes contort, bones may dislocate, people have caught fire spontaneously, levitation does rarely happen, and they have vomited bizarre things.

Q: **Is a person asking for trouble when they tinker with a Ouija board?**

A: Yes, in the sense that if the demonic world deems them useful they will use their ignorance of how things work to trick them into relying on "spirits" and "guides" until they are obeying their commands consistently. Often a person tries to cut off the communication and obedience, then the "guide" turns ugly and punishes them, showing their true colors.

Using spirit communication devices such as a Ouija board involves giving permission for an unknown spiritual entity to partly possess the body (by inviting them to use the arm and hand). The problems with spirit communication are not specific to Ouija boards; it is the act of inviting random spirits to form a relationship that is the problem.

Q: **What are the requirements for working against demons in a Catholic context?**

A: First and foremost, the religious demonologist must be called to the work by God, not by their own choice. If one wants to be a demonologist, that is a problem. No rational person wants to interact with pure evil and put their sanity, physical life, and soul at risk when they don't have to. People in this work are called into it and guided to people and situations that train them. God is in charge from the beginning to the end.

Everyone functioning along with an exorcist or demonologist must also be called to do so. There can be no bystanders or curious onlookers; they are open to being attacked and their presence is a weakness that will be used against all those present.

There must be special protection and intervention from God in order to survive, remain sane, and be effective in religious demonology. It is not the human person or the priest who drives a demon from a person's home or body. It is not the human will that makes a demon stop throwing objects around the room or causing horrible thoughts and pains in the people there. There is no personal power or authority in humans: All intervention, protection, and authority come from God on a moment-by-moment basis.

If one meddles with demonic forces without the special protection that comes from a calling from God it can lead to depression, isolation, suicidal or homicidal thoughts, obsession with demons, delusions of power or control of demons, or ultimately working for evil.

With a calling from God naturally come the contacts, friends, and guidance from people with decades of experience in this work. One cannot learn how to function as a religious demonologist from any book or website.

One must be ready to give their life to God. Death is a real possibility in this work, and that reality can be used against one to intimidate or control them if they have not surrendered to God.

One should be of a mature age. It is unhealthy for a young developing mind and soul to interact with the demonic realm. Once people cross the line into knowing the reality of demons, they go through a psychological and spiritual crisis where they must come to terms with this new reality. This can be very challenging for any adult; the young, forming mind is generally not equipped to handle this stressor successfully. Better to live a normal, happy life when young and leave this topic for later in life.

This work must be done as an act of charity and not for selfish motives like fame, money, social power, or other benefits. To do this for selfish reasons puts one in an arena with a preternatural force beyond human comprehension with little or no protection.

Q: **Should I trust information from "the dead"?**
A: The Bible clearly forbids talking to the dead (necromancy). Why is this? It is very dangerous to attempt communicating with the dead because you have no idea who or what is communicating.

Many people will say that they get information that convinces them that they are communicating with a dead relative, a helping angel, or some other entity that is "good." It is important to remember that demons can sometimes know personal things because they watch people during some of their lifetime. They can also mimic people very well, sounding just like whomever they want to.

The dead in purgatory are only allowed to ask for help or prayers, and in rare cases in resolving some sin they committed in life. They don't have permission to talk to the living beyond that. Damned souls are another matter; they are slaves to the Devil and will engage in deceptive interactions with people.

It is very tempting to believe people have special powers to hear from the dead, or that some technique or technology like EVPs can do this. Generally this is a trick of the enemy to draw people into dependence on such methods to guide their life or give them comfort, as opposed to trusting God.

Q: **Can you tell me where the Bible says I shouldn't consult the dead?**
A: Here are some references:

Deuteronomy 18:10: "Let no one be found among you who sacrifices his son or daughter in the fire, who practices divination or sorcery, interprets omens, engages in witchcraft, or casts spells, or who is a medium or spiritist or who consults the dead."

Isaiah 8:19: "When men tell you to consult mediums and spiritists, who whisper and mutter, should not a people inquire of their God? Why consult the dead on behalf of the living?"

Leviticus 19:31: "Do not turn to mediums or seek out spiritists, for you will be defiled by them. I am the LORD your God."

Leviticus 20:6: "I will set my face against the person who turns to mediums and spiritists to prostitute himself by following them, and I will cut him off from his people."

Don't be quick to dismiss these references because they are from the Old Testament and therefore "don't count." In the New Testament Jesus states that he will be our judge after death but Moses will be our accuser and will accuse us based on God's law that Moses wrote down in the Old Testament.

Q: **Should I trust information from demons?**
A: No. Demons almost always lie, telling partial truths only when it fits their manipulative agenda. They only tell the full truth under duress in exorcisms. Information from demons is almost always designed to make people feel helpless, scared, and powerless. The truth is they are powerless before God.

Q: **Can demons be redeemed and go back to God?**
A: No, they cannot. This is because they made a free will choice very different than a human free will choice: Their choice to turn away from God was made with

100 percent foresight and knowledge of the consequences. Humans are not capable of being totally aware of the truth and consequences of actions, which is partly why there is always mercy for people from Jesus. There is no mercy or redemption for the Devil and the demons because they knew exactly what they were committing to. Even if they could be accepted back by God they would not wish to be.

Q: **Can psychic sensitivity be used to find out if demons are present and their names?**

A: Almost certainly no.

Discernment is the word used to describe a spiritual gift from God that allows a person to know things they cannot know naturally. Discernment, as well as all gifts from God, is active on an as-needed basis. Generally the people that have psychic sensitivity do not have discernment. People with psychic sensitivity are generally used to it "working" all the time and being able to know what is "going on" in an area. This sometimes leads to a kind of arrogance that if they don't detect it then it's not there and no threat to them. This creates situations where they are vulnerable to being manipulated by demons. Demons can easily communicate any illusion or misinformation to a psychic sensitive without being detected for what they really are. One example of this is feeding a false name to a psychic, convincing them that they "got" the demon's name. This is to encourage people to confront or try to expel the demon with this false name, thereby overstepping their bounds. Demons never give their true name unless under spiritual duress.

Q: **How can demons be dangerous if God restricts their activity?**

A: If a person exercises their free will to knowingly confront or try to control a demon without a calling from God they bear the consequences of that choice. God doesn't violate our free will choices or the consequences of those choices.